Swarthmore Lecture 1985

STEPS IN A
LARGE R

A Quaker expl
the monastic t

by Christopher Holdsworth

QUAKER HOME SERVICE · LONDON

First published May 1985

ISBN 0 85245 188 1

Cover design by John Blamires

Printed by Headley Brothers Ltd., The
Invicta Press, Ashford, Kent and London

PREFACE

The Swarthmore Lectureship was
established by the Woodbrooke Extension
Committee at a meeting held December 9th,
1907: the minute of the Committee
providing for 'an annual lecture on some
subject relating to the message and work of
the Society of Friends'. The name
Swarthmore was chosen in memory of the
home of Margaret Fox, which was always
open to the earnest seeker after Truth, and
from which loving words of sympathy and
substantial material help were sent to fellow
workers.

The lectureship has a twofold purpose: first,
to interpret further to the members of the
Society of Friends their message and
mission; and, secondly, to bring before the
public the spirit, the aims and fundamental
principles of friends. The lecturer alone is
responsible for any opinions expressed.

The lectureship provides both for the
publication of a book and for the delivery of
a lecture, the latter usually at the time of
assembly of London Yearly Meeting of the
Society of Friends. A lecture related to the
present book was delivered at Friends
House, Euston Road, London, on the
evening of May 25th, 1985

FOREWORD

Like most forewords this one is being written last when the main text has been rewritten. I have, therefore, the happy opportunity of thanking some of those who have helped me; in the first place must come members of the Swarthmore Lecture Committee. They invited me to give a lecture—at first suggesting a theme which I have not followed—and responded to my own suggestion with great encouragement. After they received my first draft I got back many wise ideas, not all of which I have been able to incorporate, but which were a marvellous lift on the way. Jo Farrow and Clifford Barnard have acted as 'link persons' between the Committee and myself with unfailing courtesy and helpfulness. It has been altogether a strengthening experience to work with the Committee.

Secondly, I must thank four authors whose books I have used a great deal, Yushi Nomura, Henri Nouwen, Aelred Squire and Benedicta Ward. The last three I count as friends, and it was Henri Nouwen who generously sent me a copy of Yushi Nomura's book after I had stayed at Genesee. I hope they will not disapprove of my use of their work.

Beyond them are the communities at Port Glenone and Genesee who welcomed me so warmly, and brought to my heart things I had long known in my mind. This lecture is in one sense a thank offering to them.

Many others without whom I could never have written this lecture, above all my parents, are hinted at in what follows. But my present family must be thanked too: Robert for the times when we explored Narnia together, Yon for keeping me calm and happy, and Sophie for trying to interrupt, by sitting on the pages or by catching my hand with her paws.

Christopher Holdsworth
Exeter
26 February 1985

PERMISSIONS

The author and Quaker Home Service gladly make acknowledgement to the following writers and publishers to reprint from copyright sources: Sheed & Ward Ltd for the extracts from *The Rule of Saint Benedict* edited by Justin McCann; Darton, Longman & Todd Ltd for the extracts from *The Way of the Heart* by J. M. Nouwen; A. R. Mowbray Ltd for the extracts from *The Sayings of the Desert Fathers* by Benedicta Ward; SPCK for the extracts from *Asking the Fathers* by Aelred Squire; St Mary's Press (USA) for the extracts from *Praying the Psalms* by Walter Brueggemann; the SLG Press for the extract from *Exploring Silence* by Wendy Robinson; Eyre & Spottiswood Ltd for the extracts from *Desert Wisdom* by Yushi Nomura; Macmillan Publishers Ltd for the extract from *Alice through the Looking Glass* by Lewis Carroll, and William Collins, Sons & Co Ltd for the extract from *The Lion, the Witch and the Wardrobe* by C. S. Lewis. *Psalms* 4 and 91 are from the *New English Bible* published by the Oxford University Press and the Cambridge University Press.

CONTENTS

CONTENTS

I

INTRODUCTION

Looking towards the monastic tradition

My hope in the course of this lecture is to share some aspects of monastic practice and spirituality which have come to mean something to me, and which I think could enrich some other Friends. Not everyone who reads, or hears, this lecture will find it equally helpful, but I believe that there are some to whom it may be useful, and it is for them that I am concerned. But why do I imagine there is such an audience, even if I realise that I may fail to reach it because of the imperfections in what I say? Because of two separate kinds of evidence. First I know that a number of Friends regularly spend time living alongside monastic communities, become guests of monks or nuns, and that sometimes they go alone, sometimes with other Friends (occasionally such group visits surface in a short report in *The Friend*), and second, I have noticed—who has not if they have been reading Quaker journals or keeping their ears and eyes open—that there is a hunger and thirst among us for a deeper and more transforming experience of God. That inadequate three-letter word may not always be used, but I deduce that there are many who long to be found as well as to seek, to be lightened more steadily than by a very fitful faint light, to know a closer journey with that loving presence which invites us to move with it. Yet I have to admit, at the start, that the very idea of looking towards monastic communities and to the tradition in which they live, may arouse suspicions among many Friends, and that there is in the Quaker tradition quite a lot which makes it hard to see the light which may flow from them. One of the best-known passages in early Quaker writing which comes readily to mind in this connection asserts,

1

True godliness does not turn men out of the world, but enables them to live better in it, and excites their endeavours to mend it; not to hide their candle under a bushel, but to set it upon a table in a candlestick.[1]

But William Penn makes it perfectly clear in the words that precede and follow the passage, that there are sides of the Christian life to which the monastic tradition bears a faithful witness, even though he was sure that

The Christian convent and monastery are within, where the soul is encloistered from sin. And this religious house the true followers of Christ carry about with them, who exempt not themselves from the conversation of the world, though they keep themselves from the evil of the world in their conversation.[2]

Here, incidentally, he surely does not mean by conversation speech, but what the monks meant by *conversatio*, their whole walk with God.[3] I sense myself, in any case, that early Quaker criticisms of other Christians should not restrict where we look for help, since what men deny about the faith of others has less weight than what they say about their own. And I take courage from the fact that well back in Quaker history catholic spirituality was much read and used by Friends, and that within this century the direction in which I am looking would not have seemed alien to earlier lecturers in this series, like Edmund Harvey, or Rufus Jones, among those who are no longer with us, nor to Douglas Steere who writes still on themes very close to my own.[4] But perhaps it may help if I try to explain how my own experience has led me to find living words within the monastic tradition, and so to feel that these same things may speak to some other Friends too.

1 A Personal Stance

I had what I now know to be the great good fortune to be born into a home where my parents shared at the deepest level a similar outlook on life, they did not always use the same words to

2

describe it, and as they lived together they sometimes made mistakes, got out of sorts with each other or with other people. They certainly were not plaster saints, they were themselves and often it was a struggle to get through a day. But they looked in the same direction for renewal, refreshment and strength. Each night they prayed on their knees by their beds, until with age that position became too uncomfortable, and every day they read together from the Bible, or less frequently from some other book. Normally this reading took place at the end of breakfast, when father got the Bible out from the cupboard above his desk, or from a drawer in the side-board, and almost always it was he who read, after which there was a short time of quiet waiting. Very rarely was anything said in this time, though once or twice, when someone was very much on their minds, there was a brief prayer. All meals were preceded by a short silent pause. This was a pattern into which my brother and I were absorbed from the start of our lives, though we—no more I am sure than any other child in our generation—did not always find it meant a lot to us. We fidgetted during reading, later on we often rebelled against the choice of material read, and there were times when we broke the silence before meals because we wanted to get on with the main business of eating. There were times, too, when we were acutely embarrassed when our peculiar observances had to be gently explained to non-Quaker visitors. But the pattern was there, and it was only years later that I came to realise what a lot it had given to me, a familiarity with a wide range of the Bible particularly.

What I want to stress also is that it was a pattern created and sustained by two people who were devoted to the religious practices and duties of different parts of the Christian church: my mother was an Anglican (with rather middle of the road sympathies, rather than being drawn to either end of the wide Anglican spectrum), whilst my father was a Quaker and member of a family which had belonged to the Society for two generations before him, and whose older members when I was a child, still used plain speech. It is relevant that my mother had been sent to Polam Hall, then very much a Quaker institution under the guidance of Helen

Baynes. This had come about because mother had Quaker relations, in particular a step-grandmother, and since both of her parents, and also my father's mother, came from the small world of nineteenth-century Wensleydale, there were common Quaker connections. The important thing, of course, was not these connections, which did in fact make them distant relatives, but that each of them put the greatest emphasis on trying to live a Christian life, and was convinced that the regular taking part in worship, day by day, and Sunday by Sunday, was an essential part of their discipleship.

I can not recall how old I was when I was first taken to Meeting in Bolton. Normally my brother and I went there because of the children's class, whereas at the Parish church, where mother usually went, Sunday School was in the afternoon, and if children went to Mattins they were expected to sit the sermon through, which mother and father thought was asking too much of a small child. But by the time we were about eight or so we were allowed to choose where we went, either to church or to Meeting, though it was taken for granted that we would go to one or to the other. I don't think that we ever declined to go to either until we were in our teens. Sunday worship was just a normal part of every Sunday. Memory suggests that usually mother went to church, until we moved into Yorkshire, when very frequently she went to early communion and then accompanied us to Meeting.

What I want to stress here, is that from as early as I can remember, I knew that the Quaker way of attending to God was not the only way, and that the words which Friends used to describe the ways of God with man was not the only language used by religious people. Just as I came to feel a mixture of affection and frustration with what went on in the plain rectangular Meeting room, with its long benches covered with long blue cushions, and its huge, gurgling heating pipes, so I came to have similar mixed feelings about the high, dark church with its long nave, hard wooden pews, gleaming lectern, and raised-up pulpit. Silence was peaceful—one could always count the upholstery buttons if one got bored—and singing hymns was fun, and

4

occasionally, in the midst of the quiet, or the varied sounds, something seemed to happen inside me, and I felt caught up. Such an experience did not frighten me, because I somehow gathered through my parents that this happened to them too, although mother very rarely showed any visible signs of emotion, whilst father quite often, and to our embarrassment, was moved to tears. We used to pull his leg about it, and I wish now that whilst he was alive I could have thanked him for his tears, because I now know what a release they can be. What I knew, however, from as early as I can remember, was that the ineffable experience, of being caught up, could happen just as easily in Meeting as in Mattins, whilst trying to become quiet all through, or to really listen to what a Friend was saying in ministry, or whilst repeating scarcely understood prayers, or singing a favourite hymn.

This variety of experiences which mattered, developed and increased in variety at school. The life at Bootham was constructed around many of the same disciplines which I had known at home, though in the larger setting of a school and of a community in which I suppose something like two-thirds came from non-Quaker backgrounds. There was silence, not merely before, but after, meals as well, a rushed pause in the library before breakfast (when many of us were trying surreptitiously to finish dressing), school assembly every day with a reading, and on Sundays, meeting for worship at what was then called Clifford Street Meeting House, a place we also visited with the girls and staff of the Mount on Wednesday mornings for a programmed meeting with hymns and an address, rather like the evening meeting we had on Sundays at school. These were Quaker 'opportunities'. But every fourth Sunday, 'dispersed' meeting took place, when we were allowed to worship where we liked. The practice had, I think, begun as a way of keeping members of other churches in touch with the life of their own communities, but it was a chance to try other things which many of us took. So, I found myself in the Minster for Mattins with full choir, a place in which I also came to love Evensong on a Sunday afternoon, less frequently at a Methodist chapel where the music was heartfelt and warm, or at the catholic church in front of the Minster, where incense and a good deal of strange liturgical business took place before the most varied congregation which I encountered, who, like me, can hardly have found the detail of the service easy to follow, since all the prayers were said at top speed, and in Latin.

Gradually, the Quaker experiences came to feel to be the ones which meant most, so that by the time I had left school I had applied for full membership of the Society, having previously rejoiced in the now-discontinued status of a temporary member. That decision owed a lot to the many people at school and in York Meeting who made the Society and what it meant in life, real. Some were well-known names in Quaker circles, but there were others, probably unmentioned in *The Friend* except when they died, who affected me, merely by being at Clifford Street week by week, even though they remained but faces, and ones who did not speak. If there were space enough, I could say a lot about York Friends, and the staff of the two schools, but this is not the right place to do so. But one person must be mentioned, for I think he left a very large mark on me, Tom Green. An awkward, honest, searching man, with mannerisms which we delighted in imitating, he lived in a way where everything cohered, and held together as he was tried almost to destruction before our eyes, when first his wife died slowly from cancer, and then, hard close after, his eldest son was suddenly killed in Antarctica. His courageous faith shone out, so that he is one of those for whom I give thanks every time that I remember him.[5]

Cambridge which followed, after a period of alternative service to being in the army with the then Friends Service Council, was less traumatic than that last year at school, but here again I continued to find life being enhanced not exclusively in Meeting Houses. Jesus Lane, then the only meeting in Cambridge, bubbled with life. The upstairs room was often full, and every Sunday in term Young Friends met over lunch afterwards, which we took it in turns to cook, and often there was a speaker and discussion. In the evening Anna Bidder was at home, dispensing strong coffee whilst doing extraordinary things with spectacles and cigarettes, and enabling absolutely anything to be talked over. There was also the college chapel, where I usually went for Evensong on a Sunday, where first Charlie Moule, and then John Robinson, helped to create a fellowship which welcomed Christians of all traditions.[6] Under John the community which regularly worshipped together rewrote the Anglican liturgy of Holy Communion and various ways were tried to make the communion service a time when as many sides of the life of the college as possible were brought together to be redirected and enlivened. It was there that I found myself, and it seemed quite natural, taking communion, not often, nor on every occasion when I was at the communion service. And there, as at Jesus Lane, I found myself alongside a group who tried to express service for the wider community; one vacation I went on a work-camp which John had organised in Sheffield. It was at Cambridge, too, that I became a member of a small and old fellowship of Nonconformists who met together for communion and prayer each term. During these years, indeed, I became committed to closer relations between Christians of different traditions, concerned not so much with problems of organisation, as with becoming open to the richer life which such closeness could bring.

I had spent my years as an undergraduate studying History, and the fact that I am writing now of monastic things owes a lot to the two people who had the greatest impact upon me both as scholars and as teachers. First in time was Marjorie Chibnall, who tutored me for a good deal of the work I did in my second and third years, and really made the middle ages come alive. I read essays to her during my last year on subjects about which David Knowles was lecturing, in a course about the intellectual history of western Europe from about 1000 to the mid-fourteenth century.[7] Those were extraordinary lectures, perhaps the finest series I ever heard; clear, eirenic, informed with the widest reading, and delivered in a quiet, insistent voice, almost bereft of any rhetorical display, and which issued from a short, ascetic figure, always dressed in black, clerical garb. During that same year I went to a smaller seminar which he held in his rooms in Peterhouse, and came to feel that here was someone who lived in the presence of God, though there was a lot about him which I did not understand. These two teachers were the ones who really stretched my mind, and so it was, perhaps, not surprising that when after a time of hesitation, partly spent at Woodbrooke,—where two terms spent working mainly with Maurice Creasey were very helpful—I decided that I wanted to try to do research and hope for an academic career, I should turn to Dom David to ask him to be my supervisor. Nor, looking back on the way my life had travelled, was it surprising that I came to work on a group of late twelfth-century English monks and the books which they had written.

Since then, in one way and another, it has been my good fortune to be able to do something which is a continuing pleasure, despite all the times when I do not want to read another exam script, or try to produce an adequate bibliography, two of the sides of my profession which sometimes seem a chore. It has never been long before renewal has come, either through a new book, an exciting class, or the meeting and talking with another scholar.

To a certain degree the area in which I first specialised, the spirituality of the cistercians, flowed along channels which drew from some of the same sources of life as my Quaker and Anglican background had done, though there was a lot about twelfth-century monks which was quite unlike anything I had had to meet before. Oddly enough it was only recently that I spent time in living monastic communities, though I had followed in my father's footsteps as an enthusiastic visitor of monastic ruins from the time when I was a small boy; I remember still my first introduction to Fountains, on a hot day in the last summer before the war. I sometimes wonder whether I was held back from the living thing for fear that I might succumb to the 'lure of Rome', or whether in earlier days when relations between catholics and other Christians were so much more distant, it was that gap which stood in the way. But, from a host of memories, I remember with thankfulness being at the great pilgrimage church of Vézelay at the time of the patronal festival, when we walked through the streets at night singing very unQuakerly hymns, and joining in the Easter services at Assisi, including that shattering moment when the crucifix was laid on the ground. So it wasn't until five years ago when I found myself lecturing in place of a colleague at a conference in Dublin to celebrate the centenary of a teaching brotherhood, that I made friends with two cistercian lay-brothers, which led to a short visit to their house in Northern Ireland. Two years later I spent a rather longer time at one of the Trappist houses in the United States, where I was introduced by Parker Palmer, one of the staff at Pendle Hill.[8] These two experiences, short as they were, meant a great deal to me, and still have resonances, some of which you may catch in what follows.

2 Inner Space

One way of summing up my religious experience would be to say that I knew that there were various ways towards that thing which I had learnt to call the sense of the presence of God. I knew that there was just not one set of practices which led there, not merely one route with a peculiar label. From the first I knew something about the Quaker and the Anglican routes, and as I grew I came to have some awareness of others: the catholic, the Free Church and the Jewish.

It has also been true that the metaphor of a large space as the place in which we become aware of the presence has appealed to me. Perhaps this has been because as long as ever I can remember, I seem to have needed a good deal of room. One of my earliest memories is of stretching my feet down in the large old drop-sided cot we had, to feel the bottom of the bed, so to say. For a long time, too, I have been most comfortable in an extra long bed, and have needed to take care when going through doorways lest I crack my head. Besides this inbuilt attraction towards the idea of space, I also feel close to it because I have a tendency to gather clutter around, which is something which does not make it easy for those who live close to me. Tidying up, or throwing away are not things I like doing.

From early on, too, I became aware that the movement into a place where in an ineffable way God became real, was not dissimilar from what went on when I entered into the space of imagination. That kind of space was one which attracted me from as far back as I can go in memory, whether it was opened up by someone reading to me, or when I was older by my reading to myself, or by games which drew open that part of me. And I sensed that what went on when we sat round the table for reading after breakfast, or when I said my prayers before getting into bed, or when we went to worship on Sundays, belonged to the same kind of experience. Other ways into that space which opened up very early were through music, both listening to it and making it, and through the beauties of the world. Obviously now I realise that there are differences, a sense of the presence of God is not just the result of the use of imagination, or attending to something lovely, but the thing which is germane for me now, is that inner space of various kinds has called my attention and has been a large and enlivening place. It is this sense which I have tried to hint at in my title, which is derived from a phrase in the thirty-first psalm, '(Thou) hast set my feet in a large room.'[9] In various senses I am aware that my life has had a lot of space.

The sheer magic of the imaginative journey into adjacent space was never more hauntingly expressed than in the opening episode of a book with which I became familiar as soon as I was old enough to follow enough of the story as it was being read to me, *Alice Through the Looking-Glass*. Do you recall the crucial passage?[10] Alice, you will remember, had been sitting curled up in the great armchair with the little black kitten, when she began to play with it in front of the mirror;

'How would you like to live in Looking-glass House, Kitty? I wonder if they'd give you milk in there? Perhaps Looking-glass milk isn't good to drink—but oh, Kitty, now we come to the passage. You can just see a little *peep* of the passage in Looking-glass House, if you leave the door of our drawing-room wide open: and it's very like our passage as far as you can see, only you know it may be quite different on beyond. Oh, Kitty, how nice it would be if we could only get through into Looking-glass House! I'm sure it's got, oh! such beautiful things in it! Let's pretend there's a way of getting through it, somehow, Kitty. Let's pretend the glass has got all soft like gauze, so that we can get through. Why, it's turning into a sort of mist now, I declare! It'll be easy enough to get through-' She was up on the chimney-piece while she said this, though she hardly knew how she had got there. And certainly the glass was beginning to melt away, just like a bright silvery mist.

I don't suppose for a moment that I was the only small child who tried to imitate Alice and move like her through the mirror into the exciting world which lay athwart the room in which I was breathing hotly on the glass. But all I ever had to show for it was the ring of wetness which I had to hasten to rub away with my handkerchief before anyone else came into the room.

Wardrobes had a fascination for me as well as mirrors, though I didn't as a child know of them as places of transformation; rather it was the case that the rather rickety one in my bedroom always seemed to have things stored on top of it which I wanted to reach. It was, only many years later, when I had a son to read to myself, that I discovered that marvellous moment where that very solid domestic object becomes a gateway to adventure and heightened living.[11]

'This must be a simply enormous wardrobe!' thought Lucy, going still further in and pushing the soft folds of the coats aside to make room for her. Then she noticed that there was something crunching under her feet. 'I wonder is that more mothballs?' she thought, stooping down to feel it with her hand. But instead of feeling the hard, smooth wood of the floor of the wardrobe, she felt something soft and powdery and extremely cold. 'This is very queer,' she said, and went on a step or two further.

11

Time and space forbid following Lucy any further into Narnia, but I hope the point which I am trying to express about the exploration of inner space, is becoming clearer.

Before we leave Alice and Lucy it is worth observing that both the transformations took place when they *tried* to explore a space beyond the mirror or the wardrobe. I do not think it fanciful to liken this kind of attempt to that which we make when we try to find the space within, that place where God becomes more real. In the tradition which I am about to explore, that movement within was called the journey into the heart, and it is now time that we should put ourselves into a position where we can attend to some of the things which that tradition has to say about that journey.[12]

II

SAINT BENEDICT AND FRIENDS

3 Patterns and Rules

Let us begin with what the tradition has to say about the outward edges, so to say, of the journey, and then move on to what it says about the deeper movement. Most of the people whose writings and lives I have studied were monks: nuns, on the whole have left far fewer writings behind them. But the point I wish to stress here, is that they were people who lived a life directed by some general principles which they believed were derived from the Gospel. From the fifth century onwards these principles began to be written down in rules, of which undoubtedly the most significant is that attributed to an Italian, Benedict of Nursia, who lived from about 480 to 547.[13] There is a great deal about him which we shall never know, but his counsels about the monastic life, although in many places copied, without acknowledgment, from the work of an anonymous predecessor, were one of the most influential documents ever written. His Rule is simple, straight-forward and short, about twelve thousand words in the Latin original, but was early characterised as being full of sense and remarkable enlightenment.[14] The qualities which moved Pope Gregory to so call it, may become clear to us as we look at some of it. Undoubtedly its tone and manner will seem strange to readers who have not come across it before, and I would suggest that it might be read in the same way as one would try to listen to the ministry of another Friend in meeting for worship.

Benedict's over-arching aim was to create what he called 'a school of the Lord's service.'[15] By school he had in mind not so much an educational institution as a military or athletic one, but what he went on to say makes it perfectly clear that the community he wanted to establish was not a sixth-century equivalent of Sandhurst;

> Therefore must we establish a school of the Lord's service; in founding which we hope to ordain nothing that is harsh or burdensome. But if, for good reason, for the amendment of evil habit or the preservation of charity, there be some strictness of discipline, do not be at once dismayed and run away from the way of salvation, of which the entrance must needs be narrow. But, as we progress in our monastic life and in faith, our hearts shall be enlarged, and we shall run with unspeakable sweetness of love in the way of God's commandments; so that, never abandoning his rule but persevering in his teaching in the monastery until death, we shall share by patience in the sufferings of Christ, that we may deserve to be partakers also in his kingdom.

The whole idea of adopting a way of life in which there may be what Benedict calls 'some strictness of discipline' is probably not very attractive to many of us today. Brought up in the discovery methods used in primary education, sometimes (but not always) linked with ideas which value spontaneity of expression of feeling above most other things, there seems something forced and unnatural in words which are redolent with regularity, tried and tested methods and the voluntary limiting of one's own actions. But there is, if we can but recognise it, a lot in our Quaker heritage which does set store by these very things. Our two, much valued books, *Christian Faith and Practice* and *Church Government* form together the 'Book of Christian Discipline of London Yearly Meeting of the Society of Friends'. I suspect that we often forget that full description, and so that idea of discipline is not kept before our minds. Once one looks inside either of those volumes, it is not hard to find many references to disciplines, and it is interesting to speculate whether one well-loved phrase describing the qualities to be looked for in an applicant for membership, 'that he is a humble learner in the school of Christ' is an unconscious or conscious echo of Benedict's phrase.[16] Whether it be or not, it is perfectly clear that here and in the Advices and Queries, to look no further, our own guiding documents do point us towards the value of adopting a pattern of behaviour in relation to attendance at our meetings for worship and church business, and in our daily lives.[17] Yet there are Friends who recoil from the implications of our having a discipline, and turn to the lovely words of the elders meeting at Balby in 1656 (themselves placed at the end of our General Advices) for justification:

> Dearly beloved Friends, these things we do not lay upon you as a rule or form to walk by, but that all, with the measure of light which is pure and holy, may be guided; and so in the light walking and abiding, these may be fulfilled in the Spirit, not from the letter, for the letter killeth, but the Spirit giveth life.[18]

These heart-warming words, so shot-through with both the spirit and the letter of the New Testament, warn us rightly against putting our whole trust into the routine observance of any way of life, making anyone's words (however holy or old they be) a recipe for ourselves, but they are not, I believe, a warning against creating any kind of a pattern of life. And one can well imagine that most of us will not be capable of creating such patterns from nothing, out of our own heads, but will weave something fitting from the ideas of others. Certainly in our corporate life as members of a religious society we all build with the tradition which we have inherited. Not that we are thereby excused from considering whether parts of that tradition may or may not suit the needs which we sense today, but we shall have great difficulty holding together as a family of Friends if we persist in throwing everything into the melting-pot at once. I wonder, too, whether those of us who find themselves rejecting the idea of a discipline in religious matters would do so if they were trying to play the clarinet, or to dance, or to keep fit, for example. So, I hope we may be open to

15

the possibility of adopting a rule of life which may help us towards growth and may bring us more abundant life. This is a matter to which I shall return when I consider certain aspects of prayer.

Let us now pause for a moment or two at three aspects of the life in the 'school' which Benedict set up; what was promised by those who joined it, what was the chief virtue they were expected to develop in themselves, and what was the activity to which all others were to be subordinate.

'Now this shall be the manner of his reception', writes Benedict. 'In the oratory, in the presence of all, he shall promise stability, conversion of life, and obedience . . .'[19] This three-fold promise mentions first stability, a term which is not immediately intelligible to us. Almost certainly it meant two rather different things to Benedict, firstly, staying in one community, and secondly, persevering in the way of life which had been undertaken. The first kind of stability came into his mind because he knew of many monks who never settled anywhere, but were always moving on from one place to another, and so never came to terms with perseverance, stability in the second sense.[20] I do not think one needs to look far to see that in many of our lives there is a not dissimilar problem. We adopt some regular practice, say the reading of the Bible, but drop it as soon as the going becomes hard, just as many of us follow the latest set of keep-fit exercises, do them for a few weeks, and then get bored and stop doing them. I have a nice pile of guides to such exercises in my bedroom, and struggle to follow one set at the moment. It seems to me that some of those who absent themselves from meeting for worship for weeks on end may be at a rather similar sticking-point. All of us need each others' faithfulness to help us to persevere through the dry patches.

Stability, too, can mean sticking with the disciplines to which we commit ourselves when we accept membership in the Society. Each person has to find their own place within those disciplines, but our meetings for church affairs, for instance, do need support if our corporate life is to go forward. As I write this I know that there were long years during which I was but a rare attender at them, finding other activities more important. How do I explain that? Perhaps it may be that when we are most heavily burdened with responsibility, with growing children, or with demands at work, we should rightly put those first. At the other end of the situation it may be, too, that we need to do more to make those meetings more responsive to the needs which members feel, so that they become really life-enhancing times. Certainly, I believe that all of us need to keep the wider responsibilities of membership within our sights if we are to find the liberty which growing within them may bring, to know the gains of stability.

Conversion of life, on the other hand, is not so hard to understand. We, like Benedict's monks, need to let the whole of ourselves become irradiated with the Spirit, so that, in George Fox's memorable phrase, our lives 'preach'.[21] Obedience, on the other hand, is a less comfortable idea to us, perhaps because it raises, at once, the issue of obedience to what and to whom. For Benedict it certainly had these implications too; it was obedience to the Rule, the way of life chosen by the members of his community, which he believed was derived from the Gospel, and it was obedience to those who exercised authority in the community, whether they had gained it through the choice of their fellows, like the abbot, or had been given it by him, or had attained it through length of membership in the community.[22] Some of the assumptions which Benedict made about the authority vested in the abbot, that it was for life, and was ultimately something against which the monk had no appeal in this life, are very alien to contemporary thinking. It is interesting to find that many contemporary monastic communities now elect their superiors for a limited period. But it is worth realising, too, that if Benedict gives great authority to his abbot, he again and again reminds him that he will have to answer for his stewardship of the powers committed to him to God. Besides this he is counselled to take advice on many of the problems with which he has to deal, and is given clear guidance about the manner in which he should shepherd his flock. Consider, for a moment, part of the chapter on the appointment of the abbot:

Let the abbot when appointed consider always what an office he has undertaken and to whom he must render account of his stewardship; and let him know that it is his duty rather to profit his brethren than to preside over them [There is a beautiful play with words in the Latin here: sciatque sibi oportere prodesse magis quam praeesse]. It behoves him, therefore, to be learned in the divine law, so that he may have a treasure of knowledge whence he may bring forth things new and old [Here is an echo of *Matthew* 13:52]; and to be chaste, sober and merciful. Let him always *set mercy above judgement* [cf. *James* 2:13] so that he himself may obtain mercy. Let him hate ill-doing but love the brethren. In administering correction let him act with prudent moderation, lest being too zealous in removing the rust he break the vessel. Let him always distrust his own frailty and remember that the bruised reed is not to be broken [*Isaiah* 42:3]. By this we do not mean that he should allow evils to grow, but that, as we have said above, he should eradicate them prudently and with charity, in the way that may seem best in each case. And let him study rather to be loved than feared. Let him not be turbulent or anxious, overbearing or obstinate, jealous or too suspicious, for overwise he will never be at rest. Let him be prudent and considerate in all his commands; and whether the work which he enjoins concern God or the world, let him always be discreet and moderate, bearing in mind the discretion of holy Jacob who said: 'If I cause my flocks to be overdriven, they will all perish in one day' [*Genesis,* 33:13]. So, imitating these and other examples of discretion, the mother of all virtues, let him so temper all things that the strong may still have something to long after, and the weak may not draw back in alarm.[23]

There are sentiments here which all those called to serve among Friends as elders, overseers, or clerks, could well ponder upon, instinct as they are with a care for individuals and the help needed to let each person have a sense of achievement and also of there

18

still being more to strive for. That Friends as a group are now more aware of the need for our 'officers' to have some form of training and help to carry out the tasks which they have undertaken, is reflected in the courses provided at Woodbrooke and elsewhere from time to time. Perhaps the Rule could be added to reading-lists on such occasions? Certainly the whole area of obedience to the obligations which we embrace as members is a serious one. Just because we do not invest any of those who undertake office among us with obvious authority, save in the setting of the meeting for business, where the clerk may, at times, have to direct the group to bring a discussion to a close, or an individual to stop speaking so that the whole group can seek further guidance in silent waiting, we do not escape the need for each one of us to ask him or herself whether we are obedient. The question may become easier to face if we replace the word obedient with the traditional Quaker word faithful. At once the old question, supposed to have been asked by one Friend of another at the close of Meeting, 'Was thee faithful?' springs to mind. Faithfulness, in this context, I take to be the adherence to a direction sensed in the quiet waiting of worship, or to the pointers glimpsed through any experience in which God is believed to reveal his will. It involves an attempt to follow promptings which speak inwardly, it is a kind of obedience. Just as Benedict exhorted his monks to obey their abbot without delay and without murmuring—'But this obedience itself will then be acceptable to God and pleasing to men, if what is commanded be not done timorously or tardily or tepidly, nor with murmuring or the raising of objections'[24]—we need to place all our energies to the task which we find placed before us by God and to shake off all those procrastinations and half-hearted assents which so often hold us back. No doubt there is a problem in discerning whether the will of the nominations committee, for example, comes to us as the will of God which we must obey, but once we have decided to undertake what they suggest, the more whole-heartedly we can throw ourselves into it the better we shall be able to do it. As I write this I am only too well aware of what an inveterate putter off of things to a later moment and haverer I am. Perhaps in this matter we can help each other to recognise which are the leadings we ought to follow.

The one quality of life, or in his terms, virtue, to which Benedict paid most attention was humility. Chapter Seven of the Rule in which he divides humility into twelve levels, or degrees, is the longest which he wrote, and the word turns up in many other places.[25] It is, I suspect, a word which comes to us clothed with a number of displeasing overtones: in my own case they go back to Uriah Heep in *David Copperfield* with his creepy subservience. Parts of what Benedict says seem to be not entirely free of Uriahdom: his sixth and seventh levels of humility, for example are

> that a monk be content with the meanest and worst of every-thing, and esteem himself in regard to the work that is given to him, as a bad and unworthy workman . . . and that he should not only in his speech declare himself lower and of less account than all others, but should in his own inmost self believe it . . .[26]

This seems to be taking things to excess. Yet Benedict's stress becomes more comprehensible if we set it against the background of a society in which the qualities most valued were those of physical strength and bravery, and where pride in birth and inherited status were extremely significant. He was dealing with people to whom the very idea of putting other's views before one's own, or preferring the good of the community to personal advancement, was antipathetic. It occurs to me, also, that when each of us is willing to face the *prima donna* in ourselves, we may come to see humility in another light. Which of us can honestly say that we have *never* risen to our feet, having experienced what Surtees so unforgettably called 'a tremendous determination of words to the mouth', and so become convinced that the meeting, whether for worship or church affairs, just had to have the benefit of our opinions, when we might have done better to have considered them scarcely worth sharing?[27] What, too, if not about humility do the Advices speak when they recommend that we should

> Receive the ministry of others in tender and understanding spirit . . . remembering that ministry which to one may seem to have a little value, to another may be a direct word of God?[28]

The same message comes through the 'Advice to Friends concerning attendance at meetings for church affairs': paragraphs which could valuably be read by each of us before every business meeting.[29] We need, I believe, to be peculiarly humble, tender to the vision and guidance given to others, whenever we are most convinced that we are right, when just because we are so sure that we can see the way forward, we are all the more likely to lose it. The blind leading the blind was an image long ago used by Jesus, and we might perhaps place in our hands, when striding out onto some perilous edge, the question which George Fox's great contemporary, Oliver Cromwell, addressed to the stiff-necked and opinionated General Assembly of the Church of Scotland in August 1650: 'Brethren, I beseech you in the bowels of Christ, think it not possible that you may be mistaken?' Humility, in other words, is something which may indeed help us today to discover the right course of action for ourselves, and could help to oil the wheels of our corporate life. Perhaps it may give use pause, too, when, at a conference or Yearly Meeting, Friends begin to feel that they have a word for the world, which we have not always been very successful in addressing to the smaller circles around our local meetings or our homes.

But now, before leaving Benedict, let us hear what he has to say about the activity for his community to which he gave the greatest emphasis and see whether in this area he may not have a word relevant to us. The Rule devotes more chapters to the observance of corporate worship than to any other single activity.[30] Benedict is here at his most concise, yet it is possible from his directions to recreate fairly accurately what form the liturgy of his community took. Like other monastic legislators he believed that within the Bible there was good authority for rising to praise God in the middle of the night, and for joining together to do so on seven separate occasions during the day.[31] It comes as something of a surprise to find that he says very little indeed about the celebration of the Eucharist, and some modern scholars have deduced from this that Benedict, like the anonymous master whose work he adapted, may not have envisaged that his community would be an isolated community, providing for itself sacramental worship on its own, but rather that it would from time to time join in the worship of the local Christian community.[32] This point, and other details about his liturgical arrangements, need not detain us (though I shall return to consider the Psalms, which play such a large part in his scheme, later on). Instead, I want to emphasise the seriousness with which he writes of worship and of the spirit in which it should be approached. Note what he says of punctuality:

> As soon as the signal for the Divine Office has been heard, let them abandon what they have in hand and assemble with the greatest speed, yet soberly, so that no occasion be given for levity. Let nothing, therefore, be put before the Work of God [his phrase for worship].[33]

Now this, it is worth realising, is an admonition directed towards a group of people gathering together for worship eight times in every twenty-four hours; does it have anything to say to Friends who generally only worship together once a week? I would suggest that it does, for it questions the place we give to that activity in arranging our lives, and the significance we put on arriving at it on time. Let me take the second, lesser, issue first.

Admittedly the difficulties of a widely scattered group of people getting to a Meeting House on a Sunday are very different from those of Benedict's monks reaching the oratory from their work in the kitchen, or in the fields, but I think that if we find ourselves turning up week by week late, we do at least need to ask ourselves for an explanation. The virtual disappearance of public transport has certainly made the business almost impossible for many Friends, and it is certainly better to turn up late than not at all, but I suspect most of us are late for a quite different reason. We fail to set off in time; and for this failure there can be many, many reasons, particularly when young children are involved. Yet I feel that we ought to strive to be punctual, and perhaps especially when we have children. We all know how the rhythm of meeting for worship takes time to settle down, and often the process is harder when there is a trickle of late-comers making their way into the gathering group. The very need to 'centre' as soon as maybe seems to be all the greater when the younger members of the Meeting leave the larger group for their own meetings at the end of the first quarter-hour or so. These points have, of course, been made many times before, but it may be that the unfamiliarity of the way in which Benedict makes his point will help us to reconsider our own practice. Certainly he was aware of the difficulty of getting to the night office on time, and instructs his monks as they got up to 'gently encourage one another, on account of the excuses to which the sleepy are addicted.'[34] It might conceivably help if we could find a way of gently cheering each other out from our homes on Sunday mornings, without seeming superior or too serious about it.

But now let us look again at the phrase in which Benedict relates worship to all other activities. 'Let nothing, therefore, be put before the Work of God', and compare it with the place which we give to regular attendance at Sunday Meeting. It is obvious from the statistics collected a decade ago by Kathleen Slack, that many Friends *do* gather for worship week by week, but it is clear that quite a few do not.[35] Just as with punctuality we can easily recognise that real circumstances make regular sharing in worship impossible for some; family responsibilities, sickness, lack of transport, for example, may play a part. But we all know Friends who lack such impediments, and I think it is worth while considering what may hold them back.

It is exceedingly dangerous to generalise, but I feel emboldened to mention some issues in the hope that by bringing them into the open each of us may be able to do something about them.

We can, in the first place, recognise that something may be wrong at both ends of the situation, so to say, in the life of those who *do* worship regularly together, and in the lives of those who do not. No doubt it is easier for those who gather to ascribe reasons to the absentees, than to recognise the faults within themselves, so I do not intend pausing very long with those who do not come. There are times in all our lives when it is very easy to feel so burdened by the stress of living, that one decides one has so little to offer in worship, so little energy to direct one's heart and mind toward God, that it seems better to stay away, and not be present as a kind of inert weight on the group. There may, too, be some who stay away because on an occasion when they did feel distress and yet came to meeting, nothing happened—either in the meeting itself, or before or after it—which seemed helpful, nothing healed their hurt and so they may have come to nurture their feelings of dashed expectations, and even resentment, on the margins of the meeting for long periods. Those who have served as elders and overseers may know some of these. The situation may not always have had such a painful onset or outcome; worship may just have come to speak less and less to a person, or it so rarely seemed to help them to explore their inner space that they insensibly, almost inevitably, came to feel that worship was not for them. And it is at least worth wondering whether this fading out was not connected with the quality of the worship which they had shared. Let, us therefore, consider some of the things which may prevent Sunday worship coming alive.

In the first place, I believe we need to recognise that not every meeting can expect to emulate the ecstasy said to have been felt at Pentecost, to find itself transported so that the whole group feels that both words and silence are aflame with a sense of the presence of God. There may be times when something like this happens, but no group can live by 'peak' experiences alone, just as no individual can. Of course we must seek to give and receive in worship the best of which we are capable, and try to release ourselves from the things which hold us back, but the group as a whole may rarely be stirred deeply, and degrees of stirring may vary. We all know, too, from the conversations which sometimes take place after meeting, that what to one person has seemed a live meeting, to another may have seemed a scarcely live one, just as a particular piece of ministry may be a veritable word to one, and a quite unattractive mass of words to another. We are, after all, separate people moulded by varying experiences and inherited characteristics. But I have found two things helpful when a meeting has seemed very 'dry' to me: that the dryness may point to my being stuck on my inward journey, and that a dry meeting may yield life at some point in the future. For a long time I have thought of this in terms of the Emmaus story, when, you will recall, the two disciples who met with Jesus on the road failed to recognise him although they talked together about his life and death.[36] The scales only fell from their eyes when he blessed their shared supper, and it was only then that they were able to realise that their hearts had been stirred when they walked with him on the way. In a rather similar manner an arid meeting has come alive when I recalled parts of the original experience later.

I am convinced, too, that our worship is affected by the quality of the relationships between the worshippers. Here I think we tend to look the other way sometimes and to pretend that this is not the case. Every family, every pair of friends, every community, must from time to time experience strains when people get across each other, often for very trivial reasons. I remember, for example, the way I used to become exasperated by the way in which someone I loved ate salad, cutting it all up into small pieces and making a mélange out of everything in it: he also made a terrible racket eating toast. Groups experience equally trivial upsets, though sometimes the disturbances are deeper. Offence is taken at something done or said by another, and the offence is just as irritating if one party is entirely oblivious that they have done something offensive. It may be our unconscious assumptions, our deeply seated mannerisms, which get between us most awkwardly. Families, lovers, find their own ways of making up when disputes and pain have been caused, but it may be harder for members of a group, and particularly for a religious one, to find ways of becoming reconciled. Every meeting which I have known well has experienced, at one time or another, various stresses, resulting in greater or lesser pain, from the two Friends who would avoid speaking to each other, whenever possible, to those who became so alienated that they worshipped in another meeting, or refrained from public worship altogether. Why are we sometimes less than honest about these things? I sense that we dislike such 'family' disagreements because they threaten our own self-contentment; in other words, we pretend not to notice that X and Y are out of sorts with one another because we find it hard to face our own internal darknesses and, what Gregory calls 'the mind's conflicts'.[37] We are, in one way or another, unrealistic about ourselves, and others, and therefore find it hard to look for ways of taking the pain out of relationships which have gone wrong in the meeting. Our 'Book of Discipline' is not bereft of help here, and perhaps we need to be less hesitant in turning for help to those Friends who are professionally engaged in one sort of 'helping' work or another, as teachers or social workers, for instance, and who will be familiar with some of the techniques which might help us. We might, too, seek for occasions in which the disputes which divide us are assuaged and transcended in some wider celebration, or time of looking beyond local troubles.

As I have thought again about these difficulties, I reread the Rule to see whether there was anything in it which was to the point, and found there was. Benedict was very realistic about people and knew that his community was not composed entirely of those who were fully-fledged saints. How, then, did he seek to overcome animosities and estrangements? Partly by providing a hierarchy of officials whose duty it was to labour with those in their charge so that they might live up to the Rule which they had professed, and who were provided with a variety of sanctions to help them in their task, ranging from minor humiliations, to public shamings and separations, and ultimately expulsion.[38] It is hard to see an acceptable equivalent in our meetings, though our 'officers', as we have seen, do have a certain authority, and at the end of some roads there is the spectre of disownment, a spectre very rarely taken out of its cupboard these days. We would on the other hand, probably feel nearer to two other sides of Benedict's remedies for human contrariness: his enunciation of certain general principles about behaviour, and his provision of one very specific healing practice. Both of these aspects of his Rule reveal someone who faced problems very like those which trouble us.

Relevant principles occur in two places: in a chapter listing what Benedict called 'the tools of good works', and in another called 'Of the Good Zeal which monks ought to have'. The earlier chapter begins with a recollection of Christ's restatement of the commandments:

> In the first place, to love the Lord thy God with all one's heart, all one's soul and one's strength. Then, one's neighbour as oneself.

Then follows a series of short, pithy advices from which I have picked out some which seem particularly relevant to this present discussion:

> Not to yield to anger. Not to nurse a grudge. Not to hold guile in one's heart. Not to make a feigned peace. Not to foresake charity . . . Not to be jealous. Not to give way to envy. Not to love contention . . . To pray for one's enemies in the love of Christ. To make peace with one's adversary before sundown. And never to despair of God's mercy.[39]

Such 'tools of the spiritual craft' were recommended, let us remind ourselves, to a group who had chosen to live together. Benedict called a spade a spade because he realised that even within such a group men could become enemies. Perhaps his frank admission of tensions and arguments could have a useful place in the storehouse of our mind as we try to live in peace and harmony with other Friends, or indeed, with anyone.

Benedict's chapter on zeal, or enthusiasm, seems to me worth quoting in full:

27

Just as there is an evil zeal of bitterness which separates from God and leads to hell, so there is a good zeal which separates from evil and leads to God and life everlasting. Let monks, therefore, exercise this zeal with the most fervent love. Let them, that is, give one another precedence [an allusion to *Romans* 12:10]. Let them bear with the greatest patience one another's infirmities, whether of body or of character. Let them vie in paying obedience to one another. Let none follow what seems good for himself, but rather what is good for another. Let them practise fraternal charity with a pure love. Let them fear God. Let them love their abbot with a sincere and humble affection. Let them prefer nothing whatever to Christ. And may he bring us all alike to life everlasting.[40]

I hope that it will not be thought self-indulgent to quote the whole of that chapter, since parts of it almost at once open up the distance between Benedict and ourselves, a distance which in general I want to lessen. But the notes which are at once attractive, those which encourage care for one another and the practise of fraternal charity, are mixed up with ideas which do not, on the whole, so attract us; the fear of God, putting Christ first, for example, and everything being done in the hope of being led to eternal life. Yet embodied in such phrases are ideas which we need to make our own, and to the problem of their translation I shall return.

Now let us see what, beyond mere admonition, Benedict provided as a means of overcoming disputes. It was something very simple, and who is to know how well it worked—the recitation of the Lord's Prayer by the whole community at the end of Lauds and Vespers, the first and the penultimate services of the day.[41] He explains the significance of this repetition like this;

The purpose of this is the removal of those thorns of scandal, or mutual offence, which are wont to arise in communities. For, being warned by the covenant which they make in that prayer, when they say *Forgive us as we forgive*, the brethren will cleanse their souls of such faults.

28

I wonder whether this same prayer might help what one monk friend called the 'attacks of measles' which afflict us about one another? It could conceivably be useful. But prayer, as is often remarked, is rarely heard in our meetings, reflecting, I suspect, its rareness in our lives, so we probably need to rediscover prayer before Benedict's simple, yet profound provision would mean a lot to us.

Even though we may be at times aware of strains between us, I am sure that it is better to try to worship together, than to withdraw from it, provided, of course, that we go willing for reconciliation, and ready to respond to any leadings which may come to help bring it about. If, on the other hand, we go to worship in a state of tension with another Friend without being willing to find a way of reconciliation with that person, then it seems possible that the blockage will become more deeply imbedded, pushed further into ourselves and so, sadly, more difficult to remove.[42]

Such times of strain are only one of the circumstances in which we may feel so great an emptiness, pain or trouble, that we doubt whether we have any business going to meeting. I am convinced by my own experience, that these are just the moments when we should go. It was precisely when I felt at lowest ebb, when I knew that I had, so to say, no gift to take to the altar, that I found meeting had something to give me. The economy involved here is not very extraordinary, and I long ago saw it in terms of Eeyore's birthday party.[43] The bear with very little brain and his friend Piglet each remembered that it was their friend's birthday and found among their own resources something to give: Pooh, a jar of honey, and Piglet a large red balloon, splendid, cheering presents for a depressed donkey. But when they reached their friend, their gifts had undergone a radical transformation, thanks to their donors—Pooh had suddenly 'felt like a little something', and once the jar had been opened, it wasn't long before his tongue had slurped all the honey up, whereas Piglet forgetting to look where he was going, had tripped up, bursting his balloon as he fell. So the present-bearers had practically nothing to give. But do you recall how Eeyore reacted? ' "Why!" he said. "I believe my Balloon will just go into that Pot!" ' Those who have apparently little to give in meeting, do, it seems to me, give themselves to God, and to those with whom they worship, and just their very presence may release ministry in another during meeting of direct help for their need, or a helpful word, or look afterwards, so that their emptiness begins to be filled. All of us sometimes face the prospect of meeting feeling like Pooh and Piglet as they approached Eeyore in his thistle patch, but, like them, can be surprised if we make the journey. But what we never try, we shall never know.

Another aspect of this situation is expressed for me in the story of the pool called Bethesda, near the sheep-market in Jerusalem.[44] It was a place where the sick lay waiting till the ripples on the water suggested to them that an angel had passed by, who, they believed, would leave such power behind that whoever succeeded in getting into the water first would be healed. There Jesus found a man who had long been ill and yet, because he lacked someone else to carry him into the water, could never get there before anyone else. And it was him whom Jesus was moved to help and heal. But it is worth considering a moment all the others, whom Jesus did not help directly. One deduces from the story that they did have helpers, friends or relatives, who hauled them down to the brink at the right moment, and it is they who seem to me rather like us coming to worship. All of us come with various experiences from which we need to be released, things which we have done, or left undone, which we sense as soiling, weakening, but often on our own we can not summon up the strength, or open our wills wide enough, so that we can be released. Yet when we gather in worship we can draw strength from one another, and through each other and the sense of the presence of God working among the group, be enabled to let go, to be cleansed in the pool of silence. So, we need to be at meeting to help one another towards that healing place, and as we help one another, we may find our own burden being lifted.

Yet, I wonder whether the most significant thing which holds us back from going to meeting, and which affects the quality of worship once we are there, is not our lack of a spiritual discipline during the week? Thomas Green once put the matter succinctly and clearly: 'We have put upon Sunday meeting a burden which it can not stand'.[45] What he had in mind was those very weekday rituals or patterns which used to mark the lives of Friends, and in which I, like so many others of my generation was surrounded, silence at meals, family reading, private meditation and prayer. These regular times of redirection which provided release and nourishment for each individual so that he came to meeting with a store from his inward journeyings, have now well-nigh disappeared. Now, we are like Mother Hubbards who arrive at meeting to find our store is almost bare. I may be wrong in this impression. It owes a lot to the time, not so long ago, when I took part in a series of international pilgrimages of Young Friends, and used to ask how many of them came from families where silence and family reading were practised; very few answered affirmatively. A similar impression has been left on me by discussion recently at a General Meeting. It can, and should, be recognised that the old disciplines which I have mentioned sometimes took place in homes which had living-in servants, or at least regular daily help, where domestic burdens were, to some extent, lessened. Life was, too, more leisurely. But our very bustle begs a lot of questions about our priorities. I am convinced that the vitality and practical effectiveness of our Society, as of any church, is directly related to the degree to which each of us manages to find time to explore our inner space during the week. Not all of us, certainly, will find the same methods equally helpful, and different times of life may well bring changes in the ways in which we seek to know God, just as the ways in which we try to maintain our bodies in reasonable physical shape may change in the different stages of life. Rugby football may be appropriate for the youthful, skimming ducks and drakes across a pool more sensible at a later period in life. Surely it would be enormously helpful if we were readier to share with one another our discoveries in this area, for without some growth here we shall fail to respond as constructively as we might to the opportunities which are before us. In the second half of my lecture I want to turn towards the monastic tradition for help in our private and family growth towards spiritual maturity.

4 Delaying and growing with the Bible

It is abundantly clear from Benedict's Rule that corporate prayer, the daily recitation of the Office, took place in the midst of a life in which every activity, from eating to working with the hands, or with the mind, was supposed to contribute towards the creation of a holy community, his school of the Lord's service. One of the activities for which he provided plenty of time each day was what he called sacred reading, *lectio divina*.[46] He did not think it necessary to describe what he meant by this, presumably because in his day the words were so much a part of the common language that they needed no explication; he used them rather in the same way that a Friend speaking to a Quaker audience might refer to the Inner Light and feel no need to translate into a more extended and descriptive phrase. So it is necessary for us to look elsewhere to find what *lectio divina* meant.[47]

Primarily within the monastic tradition *lectio divina* meant the reading of the Bible, the *divina pagina*, those Scriptures which were held to embody the word which the attentive reader might hear as he read. Indeed he would hear, in an obvious sense too, since reading in the ancient world, and for much of the middle ages, involved making a noise; it was not a silent activity, but gave rise to sound. The explanation for this may lie in the kind of hand-writing in which books were written which involved something very akin to speed-writing: many words were drastically abbreviated, and there were special signs to indicate where certain letters had been left out. Reading involved far more than running the eye over type does today, and it is not surprising that as the reader moved his eye along the line, the tongue and larynx combined to murmur. The whole process of transferring signs on the page into a form where they could be apprehended in the mind, was almost certainly noisier than would be tolerated in any library nowadays,

32

and it may well have been fairly slow. It is hard to realise just what reading in that manner may have been like, and what effects it had on comprehension. Certainly it must have been as removed from some of the quick reading methods now taught as it is possible to imagine. In the case of the Bible further differences from the methods we usually employ now were extremely significant.

Although some attention to the meaning of the text—what the actual words signified—was normal, this was not the aim of the exercise. A monk might, for example, consult well-known and widely-available works by Jerome to understand the geography of Palestine and the meaning of its place-names, very occasionally an individual might have acquired sufficient knowledge of Greek to be able to compare the Latin Vulgate, the version which he would be most likely to have to hand, with the Greek original of the New Testament, or with the so-called Septuagint, the translation into Greek of the Old Testament. But most of the monastic reader's energy was spent trying to find a word within the words, a live word for him. The aim was not to get to the end of a certain portion of the book within a certain amount of time, but to arrive through reading to a place where God was revealed through the reading. In a sense the words he was reading became a means of exploring towards God, and when the inner voice took over, then prayer and silence might take hold so there was no need to read any further. Sometimes the whole process was called rumination and likened to the way in which some animals chew their cud. Or it was called savouring, reaching the inner flavour which lay within the words. Making the words of Scripture their own was a process to which monks were recommended to bring all the resources of their imagination; to consider what an incident had looked like, what sounds and smells had been there, so that the reader was brought into the scene himself. We can see the effects of this method in many of the commentaries which they wrote upon the Bible. There, too, they drew upon all the possibilities of language to try and bring their readers into a present experience which would involve the whole personality. Sometimes this led to what seem now rather artificial uses of rhetoric, including rather stylised dialogues with characters in the Bible. All this is very unlike the ways of reading the Bible to which we are accustomed today, those made familiar by the literary-critical school of Biblical scholars, but they are not so unlike the methods recommended in a modern book like *Transforming Bible Study* by Walter Wink.[48]

This leisurely, imaginative approach to the Bible seems to me to be attractive and has enabled me to rediscover the Bible, which, to a certain degree, an early introduction at school to form criticism, had distanced. By this I do not mean to imply that the scholarly study of the Bible is not important, we need to face the challenges and insights which it brings, but whereas few of us can attain a scholarly understanding of it, all of us can use the Bible as a jumping-off point for our exploration of the space in which we are met by God. Certainly I do know that the monastic way of reading the Bible has helped me to use my imagination as I read, and this is a faculty which so many sides of modern life combine to atrophy. The strength of these forces was well summed up in 1928 by D. H. Lawrence in an essay written on the influence of *Hymns in a man's life* for a newspaper. There he said:

> Now the great and fatal fruit of our civilisation, which is civilisation based on knowledge, and hostile to experience, is boredom. All our wonderful education and learning is producing a grand sum total of boredom. They are bored because they experience nothing. And they experience nothing because the wonder has gone out of them. And when the wonder has gone out of a man he is dead. He is henceforth only an insect. When all comes to all, the most precious element in life is wonder. Love is a great emotion and power is power. But both love and power are based on wonder. Love without wonder is a sensational affair and power without wonder is mere force and compulsion.[49]

Perhaps the point is made too stridently, but I imagine that if Lawrence were writing today, he would see many more signs of the loss of wonder in our society. And surely it is right to believe that the Bible will only come alive to us when we approach it with our imaginations and so make some of it our own, important as it is to try to appreciate what scholars have to say about it too.

The monastic tradition of *lectio divina* has, I am sure, more to share with us about the Bible, and I would like to mention now two other things it has given to me. I was, happily, brought up by parents who set great store by the Bible, but there were parts of it which we rarely or never read, perhaps because they were felt to be irrelevant or unedifying. Now, thanks to monks, I have had my taste widened, though there are still some parts of the Bible which are pretty opaque to me. All that has happened, is that I have come to see that the Bible is about people, every kind of situation is there, and many of their struggles are not so unlike our own— scarcely a very startling discovery, you may remark! Gregory the Great, the man who sent Augustine to bring Christianity to the people of Kent in 597, and a near-contemporary of Benedict's, put the whole matter succinctly:

> Holy Scripture is set before our minds like a mirror, that we may see our inward face in it. It is there that we may come to know our ugliness and our beauty. There we realize what progress we are making, how far we are from improvement. It tells of the doings of holy ones, and stimulates the hearts of those who are weak to emulate them. For as it records their successes, it strengthens our fraility in our struggles against the vices. Its words have the effect that our mind is less afraid in its conflicts for seeing the histories of so many brave men set before it. Sometimes, however, it not only tells us of their virtues, but also reveals their falls. In the successes of the strong we see what we ought to aim at imitating; in their falls what we should fear. Thus Job is described as raised up by temptation, but David brought to ground by it.[50]

The Bible is not a collection of lives of the saints, not everyone comes to a good end, and those that do have often passed through some pretty rough places. But it is just this which makes it a mirror which I may use to understand more about myself. The monastic approach is summed up in another passage which I want to pass on; it was written by a twelfth-century follower of Benedict, William of St Thierry:

> Further, you should spend certain periods of time in specific sorts of reading. For if you read now here, now there, the various things that chance and circumstance send, this does not consolidate you, but makes your spirit unstable. For it is easy to take such reading in and still easier to forget it. You ought rather to delay with certain minds and grow used to them. For the Scriptures need to be read in the same spirit in which they were written, and only in that Spirit are they to be understood. You will never reach an understanding of Paul until, by close attention to reading him and the application of continual reflection, you imbibe his spirit. You will never arrive at understanding David until by the actual experience you realise what the psalms are about. And so it is with the rest. In every piece of Scripture, real attention is as different from mere reading as friendship is from entertainment, or the love of a friend from a casual greeting.[51]

For William we know that friendship meant a great deal, his relationship with Bernard of Clairvaux changed his life, and so to find him relating reading the Bible to friendship says much. Friends will remark, too, how close part of what he writes is to the things that early Friends held about the way in which the Bible could be understood. One may set his sentence 'For the Scriptures need to be read in the same spirit in which they were written, and only in that spirit are they to be understood', besides two statements, the first from George Fox, the second from James Naylor:

> 'For I saw in that Light and Spirit which was before Scripture was given forth, and which led the holy men of God to give

them forth, that all must come to the Spirit, if they would know God or Christ or the Scriptures aright, which they that gave then forth were led and taught by'.

'. . . and none can rightly understand the Scriptures, but they who read them with the same spirit that gave them forth . . .'[52]

Early Friends, in this sense, were inheritors of a long tradition, which in the early middle ages had been developed in monasteries, that reading the Bible aright was dependent upon coming into contact with the living guidance of the Spirit, which had been behind the experiences of those who wrote the Biblical record. I doubt whether Fox or Naylor were aware of their indebtedness, but it does look as though they drew on the same fount as William of St Thierry.

5 Moving through the Psalms

These generalisations about a way to read and experience the Bible may be made more vivid if I attempt an example of such reading in action. I have chosen to do so by looking at two of the three Psalms which the Rule sets for Compline, the last service of the monastic day, namely number four and number ninety-one.[53]

I have made the choice of two Psalms, rather than one Psalm and a passage from another part of the Bible, because the book of Psalms was one in which not so long ago I read little myself: I had my favourites there to which I returned again and again, the twenty-third, or the hundred and twenty-second, for example, but much of the Psalter was a closed book to me. Parts of the difficulty which I had with it were I imagine not peculiar to me, and so I hope that sharing them, and the ways in which they have come to seem not so much problems as opportunities, may be helpful to others.

As a child the Psalms first impinged on my consciousness in the setting of Mattins, when I was often completely at sea trying to fit

37

the words in the book to the chant being sung. There seemed to me then a good deal about the exercise of what I discovered Friends tended to stigmatise as 'vain repetition', though occasionally a phrase struck home. At school Tom Green used to read them quite often in assembly, whilst at home they used to appear in reading from time to time. But I only came to look at them with new eyes relatively recently; the changes occurring when I first visited a live monastery.

Long before that happened, as soon as I began to read works written in medieval monasteries when I was a research student, I realised that the part of the Bible which had most evidently affected what I was reading, was the book of Psalms; phrases from it occurred frequently, and allusions to, or reminiscences of it, were widespread. Although I knew, with the top of my head, that the monastic tradition of corporate worship was built around the Psalms, so that, for example, according to Benedict's arrangements, the whole Psalter was repeated every week, the significance of this had not really hit home until I observed monastic life at first hand. Then, as I joined in the singing of the Psalms to very simple chants which were broken by long silent pauses at the end of each verse, enabling one to concentrate on the words, I gradually realised how it was that monks became so soaked in the Psalms that monastic writers would naturally shape their ideas around the Psalms. And, parts of the Psalter came alive for me in a new way. It was during my second visit to a monastery that I was lucky enough to be directed towards a short book, *Praying the Psalms* by Walter Brueggemann.[54] This has helped me enormously, and it will be obvious to those who do know his book how much what follows owes to his ideas. He it was who brought home to me three things about the Psalms: they have always been used by Christians of all kinds, not just by monks, as a vehicle for prayer, both in corporate worship and in individual prayer; they have also been so used by Jews; and Jesus as a faithful Jew did so too, drawing on them repeatedly during his life, from the time of the Temptation until his death. Now, after that preliminary word let us turn to the two Psalms which I have chosen.

Psalm 4

Answer me when I call, O God, maintainer of my right,
I was hard pressed, and thou didst set me at large;
be gracious to me now and hear my prayer.
Mortal men, how long will you pay me not honour but
    dishonour,
or set your heart on trifles and run after lies?
Know that the Lord has shown me his marvellous love;
the Lord hears when I call to him.
However angry your hearts, do not do wrong;
though you lie abed resentful, do not break silence:
pay your due of sacrifice, and trust in the Lord.
There are many who say, 'If only we might be prosperous
    again!
But the light of thy presence has fled from us, O Lord'.
Yet in my heart thou hast put more happiness than they
    enjoyed when there was corn and wine in plenty.
Now I will lie down in peace, and sleep;
for thou alone, O Lord, makest me live unafraid.

Psalm 91

You that live in the shelter of the Most High
and lodge under the shadow of the Almighty,
who say, 'The Lord is my safe retreat,
my God the fastness in which I trust';
he himself will snatch you away
from fowler's snare or raging tempest.
He will cover you with his pinions,
and you shall find safety beneath his wings;
you shall not fear the hunters' trap by night
or the arrow that flies by day,
the pestilence that stalks in darkness
or the plague raging at noonday.
A thousand may fall at your side,
ten thousand close at hand,

but you it shall not touch;
his truth will be your shield and your rampart.
With your own eyes you shall see all this;
you shall watch the punishment of the wicked.
For you, the Lord is a safe retreat;
you have made the Most High your refuge.
No disaster shall befall you,
no calamity shall come upon your home.
For he has charged his angels
to guard you wherever you go,
to lift you on their hands
for fear you should strike your foot against a stone.
You shall step on asp and cobra,
you shall tread safely on snake and serpent.
Because his love is set on me, I will deliver him;
I will lift him beyond danger, for he knows me by my
   name.
When he calls upon me, I will answer;
I will be with him in time of trouble;
I will rescue him and bring him to honour.
I will satisfy him with long life
to enjoy the fulness of my salvation.[55]

   The first thing that is worth observing about these Psalms is that
in both of them there are changes of audience and of speaker, the
addressor and the addressee do not stay the same throughout as
one might expect. In Psalm 4 there are four (or five) such changes
in sixteen lines. The first three have God as their recipient, but
then, quite suddenly, without any explanation comes the first
change, a reply from God for two lines. Then, at greater length
over four lines, the writer declares his faith and gives some advice
to others (second change), and next imagines some people pro-
testing how God has deserted them (two verses, and possibly
third change), and the Psalm ends with the writer communing
again with God (fourth change). The variation is not so frequent
in the much longer Psalm 91: most of it is addressed to an unspec-

ified 'you', and then, again as in Psalm 4 without any break, in the last seven lines the Lord himself speaks of those who have put their trust in him to the psalmist. These Psalms are not monologues, but dialogues at least, sometimes with more voices.

But what does this matter, why is it worth remarking? Well, it surely shows that for the psalmist God was at least someone who could be addressed, and whom it was not inappropriate to imagine replying. His universe was not deaf, nor unable, in some sense, to be in touch with the divine. A real conversation was possible, in which, as we shall see, everything could be brought into the presence of God.

Indeed, as we look at the subject matter of the dialogue, we can see that the psalmist was not interested in producing an easy, cheery, pink and white complexioned, exchange, but rather in bringing out into the open deep fears, as well as hopes. Note, for example, the striking move from confidence in God to an attempt to reassure those who feel anything but confident in him, but are full of anger and resentment:

> Know that the Lord has shown me his marvellous love;
> the Lord hears when I call to him.

and then,

> However angry your hearts, do not do wrong;
> though you lie abed resentful, do not break silence;

The dark feelings are not ignored, they are recognised as there, and the psalmist encourages the reader not to let them rip, but to transform them by worship and commitment to God;

> pay your due of sacrifice, and trust in the Lord.

Again and again in the Psalms we find a similar recycling of misdirected feelings, which comes with added force because the writer/singer also makes it clear that he, too, has been at the end of his tether (the great metaphor is 'in the pit'), but even so has been pulled out of it by God.[56]

I find this kind of confident realism extremely helpful; the

41

darkness which we all feel from time to time is not denied, as though it did not exist, but it is asserted that even that dark is not without its light.

I do not find it so easy to go along with the way that the psalmist becomes excited by the thought of the nasty fate which will befall those with whom he is at enmity. Psalm 91 presents us with this voice which grates on the ear, in the middle. Whereas the opening of the Psalm is full of grace and strength, then comes the metaphor of battle, and we are brought up in our stride:

> A thousand may fall at your side,
> ten thousand close at hand,
> but you it shall not touch;
> his truth will be your shield and your rampart.
> With your own eyes you shall see all this;
> you shall watch the punishment of the wicked.

Some of the Psalms are almost wholly given over to this expression of the desire for vengeance and the death of enemies. What do we do with such Psalms or such verses? Certainly in the past I used to mentally switch off when faced with them in a liturgical setting, and skipped them when reading on my own. I was, therefore relieved to find in the monastery at Genesee, that many in the community had felt the same, to the extent that they had marked in their service books certain Psalms to be omitted. But by the time of my visit, they were back to the Psalms uncensored and entire, largely because, I was told, that they had become convinced that the vengeance psalms have a real use. They help to bring to the surface feelings which all humans have, and which need, like everything else, to be offered to God for transformation. The Psalms do not encourage the singer or reader to take vengeance himself, but leave it to God. Brueggemann has some pages on these Psalms which are very much to the point.[57] I commend them warmly, however surprising you may think it to bring the dark sides of ourselves into the light. In my experience there is no substitute for facing the hurts which we think that others have done to us, or which we know we have done to ourselves. These times when we have been pained often fester as we refuse to recognise them, and instead, so to say, nurture them within. But if we can somehow manage to verbalise them into our own despairing song, some of the pain begins to lift. It is as we hear ourselves presenting our feelings, warts and all, before the deeps that we gain, too, a sense of perspective; what we had feared to acknowledge and pushed down into our subconscious, comes out into a healing light, and begins to be changed.

The other feature of the Psalms which Brueggemann helped me to appreciate, and so to use more fully in my own explorations of interior space, is the way that they move in metaphors.[58] The Psalms are not made up of logically connected statements made in neutral, descriptive language: they are written in verse, and like much poetry call upon many of the resources which heighten language and make it strike home. They are often shaped in parallel phrases, or use significant repetitions, but the device which occurs most frequently is metaphor. Look, for example, at the opening of Psalm 91 again:

> You that live under the shelter of the Most High and lodge under the shadow of the Almighty . . .

Here we have the metaphor that God has a shadow, and as we stay with the words we can see how they suggest something very deep, just because God is here related with something which we all know and have observed. The Psalmist does not attempt to define what being 'shadowed' by God is, instead he uses language in such a way that each person can freely use their own experience to make the words live. Brueggemann says this so well that I must quote him here:

> Metaphors are quite concrete words rooted in visible reality but yet are enormously elastic, giving full play to imagination in stretching and extending far beyond the concrete referent to touch all kinds of experience. The meaning of the metaphor is determined not only by what is there but what we bring to it out of our experience and out of our imagination.

The work of prayer is fully to explore and exploit the metaphor in terms of our own experience.[59]

He illustrates the generalisation by exploring the 'table' in Psalm 23, but it seems more appropriate now if I move back and fro through the metaphors in two verses of one of the Psalms we have already been looking at, Psalm 91.

He will cover you with his pinions,
and you shall find safety beneath his wings.[60]

Pinions, those small feathers at the edge of a bird's wings, bring to my mind the marvellous way that a hawk, for example, stands in the air, each part of its attention poised, stretched out to the very tips of its wings, in electric, silent stillness, watching, waiting. Again, pinnions conjure up that magical sound with which Handel introduces the angels converging above the shepherds outside Bethlehem, when as fluttering arpeggio follows arpeggio, we seem to hear the trembling wings, whilst the solo voice declaims,

And suddenly, there was with the angel a multitude of the heavenly host . . .

Those wings remind me too as I write these lines during the Christmas season, of that carol in which Gabriel's wings as he approached Mary are said to have been like 'beaten gold', his eyes 'like flame'.

So far, the metaphors have brought to mind experiences of attention, of unexpected arrival, of marvellous greeting, and as I read the words again I can glimpse something meaningful about the way God may reveal himself to me. But the wings and the safety beneath them evoke a closer, warmer experience. As a very small child, when staying with my grandparents, in the country, I was taken to feed the chickens in their coop on the grass. I saw the hen gathering them together under her warm breast, shuffling them beneath the protection of her feathers so that they would not suffer from the cold. And this refreshes and enlivens the way in which I imagine that God cares for me. To quote Brueggemann again,

> Metaphors, are not packaged announcements; they are receptive vehicles waiting for a whole world of experience that is itself waiting to come to expression. And if in the praying of the Psalms, we do not bring the dynamic of our own experience, we shall have flat, empty prayers treating the language as one-dimensional description.[61]

This way of understanding metaphor, of course, helps us to understand a great deal of the Bible, as it does, too, the writing of early Friends, drenched as they were in the water of Scripture. They inevitably and naturally wrote and spoke in metaphors. What, for example, is the light, but a sublime and liberating metaphor?

Before we leave the Psalms, let me refer to Brueggemann once more, to a passage which ties together what I have been trying to say about reading the Bible, and about the help we may obtain from the monastic tradition of *lectio divina*, with prayer about which I shall soon write. He explains,

> The Psalms, do not insist that we follow word for word and line by line, but they intend us to have great freedom to engage our imagination toward the Holy God. Our listening mostly moves in and out by a free association of ideas. Whether we plan it or not, are permitted or not, we will take liberties as the Psalm passes by to move out into the richness of our experience and then back into the awesome presence of God. That is the way of metaphors. They are not aisles down which we must move; they are more like rockets which explode in ways we cannot predict, causing some things to become unglued and creating new configurations of sensitivity. Like the rockets, if we are attentive, they may both shatter and illuminate. The Psalms are our partners in prayer. Such evocative language permits both partners a marvellous freedom with which to surprise the other.

45

Thanks to Brueggemann and my monastic friends, I am just starting to realise how powerful the Psalms are, in providing us with rockets to lift us up, where we can see our experience in a new light, become unglued, and from which we return to ourselves more determined to grow and mature.

III

THE FATHERS AND OURSELVES

6 The Lives of the Fathers

Benedict, as we have seen, wrote little in his Rule about *lectio divina*, and to discuss what he meant we have had to look wider in the monastic tradition, and then been led beyond to a modern scholar whose ideas are entirely in accord, at the points where we have looked, with that tradition. The search led us to that merging of reading and prayer, and it is now towards the exploration of inner space by prayer that I want to turn. Here Benedict has little directly to say, either, but he points quite clearly in this case to where he expected his monks would find guidance. In the last chapter of his Rule, he advises those who want to progress beyond what he calls 'the rudiments of monastic observance' to look to the 'teachings of the holy Fathers', among which he specifies 'the Conferences of Cassian and his Institutes, and the Lives of the Fathers, as also the Rule of our holy father Basil'; 'What else are they', he asks, 'but tools of virtue for good-living and obedient monks'.[62] Now it is particularly to the tradition represented in his list by the 'Lives of the Fathers' that I want to turn for help, since it, like the monastic tradition of reading the Bible, seems to me to be full of sense and real practical help.

The 'Lives of the Fathers' was one of the collections of stories made about the first men and women (for there were Mothers as well as Fathers) who moved out from the populous parts of the eastern mediterranean into the deserts of Egypt and Asia Minor in the fourth century. These stories have a very complicated history, but, fortunately it need not worry us now.[63] What is significant, however, is that they originated in words of advice which were given by men or women to particular people who had

47

consulted them. These 'life-giving words' first given to individuals, and felt by them to be a veritable aid to salvation, were treasured and collected because they were also found to answer the needs of others. And in one form, or another, these stories were used again and again in monastic history just because they were found to be so helpful. Within this century they have found a wider life beyond monastic circles as they have been translated into the vernacular.[64]

Three inter-related matters illustrated in these stories have been helpful to me; the necessity for solitude, for silence, and for attention towards God.[65] In one sense these three aspects are all different sides of the same thing: just what it is will I think emerge if we attend to the Fathers.

7 Solitude

The early ascetics were driven out into the desert because they believed that there they could find God, and learn to love and serve him effectively.[66] They looked to the desert because it was, so to say, all around them, near at hand to the narrow strips of cultivable land on either side of the Nile, or around the great oases. They also went there because they knew that it was the place where Jesus had gone, and where many of the great Jewish leaders—Moses and Elijah, for instance—had sought God. The attraction of the desert and the liberation it brought them comes across in a simple story. A monk called Amoun met another older man, Sisoes whom he found sad,

> because he had left the desert. Abba [the title does not mean an abbot, but something more like the Father used of some priests] Amoun said to him, 'Abba, why grieve about it? What would you do in the desert, now that you are so old?' The old man pondered this sorrowfully and said to him, 'What are you saying to me Amoun? Was not the mere liberty of my soul enough to me in the desert?'[67]

Liberty of soul meant the possibility of facing the many aspects of an individual's life which kept him from God, and was a process which the stories very often describe in terms of a battle, picking up the metaphor from the Old and the New Testaments. The struggle with inward compulsions, whether greed for money, power or sexual release, is often told in terms of fighting with devils, a personification in harmony with the ideas of the time, but one we find hard to understand.[68]

It is, perhaps, easy to dismiss the value of their experiences for two different reasons; that they were fighting against themselves in what seems to us to be an unhealthy way, and that their struggle is irrelevant for us just because they had retreated from the world. Certainly, those who went to the desert had rejected for themselves the ties of family life, and, therefore, many experiences which would seem good and natural to us. But they believed that this what they were called to, was a part of their following of Jesus, and in their new setting took very seriously their obligations to the brothers and sisters whom they had found. It is also true, I think, that the stories of the early days do not show people who went in for feats of competitive asceticism, or who were obsessed by what they called 'impure thoughts'. Later in the sixth century, such things are found, but they are not typical of the earlier period. Among the second or third generation of desert dwellers the wisdom of the beginnings was somewhat narrowed and accentuated; just the kind of development which can be observed in the history of our own Society, where, for example, the concern for plainness became an obsession with particular styles in garments and furnishings. As for the permanence of their retreat, it is probably natural for us to think that they mistook their guide; we would prefer that they, like Jesus, had returned to the world to serve it, after a time in the desert had prepared them to serve it better. Yet the stories make two things very clear; that the world was never far away, rarely more than a day's walk, and that those who dwelt in the desert, on the fringe of society, were constantly receiving visitors and helping them with advice. There is much, too, about the world of the fourth century which helps to explain their attitude. Society had rapidly embraced Christianity, following in the steps of the emperor Constantine, and those who retreated from it felt that the faith had in a real sense been diluted as what Augustine called the 'host of good and bad fishes' were swept into the nets of the church. Our world is a very different place, and yet I do not doubt that we need the witness from the desert and to find some equivalent in our own lives.

Many of us live at such a pace, where we almost boast that we never have a spare moment, that we can go for long periods without ever having time for solitude and the challenges which it brings. The lure of activity may be peculiarly hard for Friends to resist, because so often we are, apparently, capable people who have much to do and to give, both in our work and in our service to the Society. A public Friend, as they used to be called, can very easily spend most of his or her time dashing from one good cause to another, but I doubt whether any of us can in fact do without some solitude. It is abundantly clear that Jesus needed it, and I see no reason why we should not. Sometimes it needs some accident, or personal disaster, a bereavement for instance, to bring us to our senses, and to the place where we can take stock. Quite what form solitude will take for each of us, surely will vary; for one it may be a solitary walk, for another a time alone at home: some will need to make a desert in each day, others may make spaces in holidays or at some weekends.

If we go out into our desert the layers of ourselves which are obscured during our busyness will come to the surface; it is stupid to pretend that they won't. All the stupid, unsatisfactory, unlovely sides of ourselves which we often think are not there, will work their way up and have to be faced. It is cheering to find that there were men in the desert who were as deluded as we often are;

A brother came to Abba Poemen and said, 'Abba, a variety of thoughts are coming into my mind and I am in danger'. The old man took him out into the air and said, 'Open your robe and take hold of the wind'. And he answered, 'No, I

50

cannot do it'. The old man said, 'If you cannot do it, neither can you prevent thoughts from coming in. But what you should do is to stand firm against them'.[69]

Poemen gave brisk advice to the brother, as do many of the stories, but they also make clear, beyond any doubt, that those who undertake the transformation of themselves can achieve nothing if they do not somehow or other, find strength beyond themselves in the encounter. The desert dwellers come to us as men and women who went out to meet someone, and they had no hesitation in calling him Christ. They didn't always remember him, or fix their minds in his direction, but when they did, they experienced a liberation from the struggle with their darker selves. Abba Elias told a story to illustrate this;

> An old man was living in a temple and the demons came to say to him 'Leave this place which belongs to us', and the old man said, 'No place belongs to you'. Then they began to scatter the palm leaves about [which he would be using to make baskets and ropes for sale], one by one, and the old man went on gathering them together with perseverance. A little later the devil took his hand and pulled him to the door. When the old man reached the door, he seized the lintel with the other hand, crying out, 'Jesus, save me'. Immediately the devil fled away. Then the old man began to weep. Then the Lord said to him, 'Why are you weeping?' and the old man said, 'Because the devils have dared to seize a man and treat him like this'. The Lord said to him, 'You had been careless. As soon as you turned to me again, you see I was beside you'.[70]

The thought that Christ will be met in this solitude, may present a major barrier to some of those who have read so far; it may seem to show that there is not much here for use in their search for meaning in life, or whatever words they use instead of God. I think that solitude is helpful to all of us, whatever formulations we use to describe our beliefs, and, I would, therefore, be sorry if anyone was put off using it because of the way that the desert dwellers described their experience. Yet, it has to be admitted that here I have come to a place where I can only say that this is what the Fathers say, and that in my own very halting way, I have found the same. It would be inappropriate to attempt to argue a case here, I am not trained as a theologian, and the whole exercise would take up too much space. Neither do I wish to appear to judge those whose beliefs differ from my own, but it does seem to me that what the desert tradition says here, accords both with the central Christian tradition, and with what the Society of Friends has said. The conviction in the last story, that Christ was with the man struggling with his darkness, with the attraction towards the things which he wished to overcome in himself, means to me that in his struggle he suddenly realised that all was not over, that Jesus was with him. He felt this, partly because he knew of the struggles which Jesus had had with his own inner demons in the time of temptation, and at times of tiredness and distress during his life, at Gethsemane and on the cross. So in his struggle, the monk felt beyond any doubt that somehow in the strange economy of life, Jesus was there with him; just as Jesus had laboured himself, he now was with his follower. The monk could have been wrong, he may have been deluded, just as may those be who say that they have never known an experience of Christ's presence: each person must live as best as they can, trusting that they will grow and be changed, and come to fuller light as life proceeds. And in some respects, what people say about their experiences is less important than what sort of people they become, than how they act, as Jesus himself reminded his disciples.

There certainly is a clear message from the desert which relates to this issue. Solitude, it is made clear in many stories, should not produce people who worry about judging others, but instead should create individuals who are full of compassion, just because they have come face to face with their own weaknesses. The first point is made many times in these stories, and may be illustrated by two very short ones:

Abba Xanthias said, 'A dog is better than I am, because it also has love, but it does not pass judgment'.[71]

Or again, Abba Moses said,

> 'If we are on the watch to see our own faults, we shall not see those of our neighbours. It is folly for a man who has a dead person in his house to leave him there and go to weep over his neighbour's dead'.[72]

Putting the point of this second story another way, would be to say that it is useless judging others for their failures when we have failed to face our own. And perhaps, the wide-spread impression that the Society of Friends is made up of 'good' people, is one of the most powerful deterrents we could have invented to prevent people joining us in our search for life, and life more abundant. We need to face ourselves if we are to show the kind of love which does not condemn but release. The kind of compassion we need is indicated in another story about Abba Ammonas, a disciple of Anthony. It was said of him that in his solitude he,

> advanced to the point where his goodness was so great that he took no notice of wickedness. Thus, having become bishop, someone brought a young girl who was pregnant to him, saying, 'See what this unhappy wretch has done; give her a penance'. But he, having marked the young girl's womb with the sign of the cross, commanded that six pairs of fine linen sheets should be given her, saying, 'It is for fear that, when she comes to birth, she may die, she or the child, and have nothing for the burial'. But her accusers resumed, 'Why did you do that? Give her a punishment'. But he said to them, 'Look, brothers, she is near to death, what am I to do?' Then he sent her away and no old man dared accuse anyone any more.[73]

8 Silence

It may seem otiose, if not downright stupid, to talk to Friends about silence. We alone (we sometimes think) among Christians regularly use it in our corporate worship. Ministry sometimes occurs when thanks for this gift are given in such a tone to remind one of the way in which the Pharisee prayed at the temple. But, although we use silence as the medium through which we become aware of the divine presence, and of one another, it is our way of communion, there are many indications, as we have seen, that we do not make a quiet place in our daily lives. Certainly we, like all those who live alongside us in Britain today, or, indeed in any part of the developed world, live in an environment which is polluted by noise. The roar and honking of traffic, the invidious soupyness of muzak in shops, offices and factories, the clatter of machinery. Thanks to the wonders of modern batteries and the silicon chip, transistors can suddenly be produced from a pocket, or a hand-bag, filling a lonely beach, or a high hill with noise. We are in danger of drowning in noise. And we are also assailed on every side by words, not always spoken out loud, but leaping at us from hoardings and newspapers, from television and radio. Both tire, and also, as D. H. Lawrence reminded us earlier, bore, so that many of us are not easily able to stand silence, or to still the incessant chatter within our minds.[74] Let us now turn to the desert to see whether it can help us with these problems.

In the desert, where most of the sounds which we take as normal were lacking, and where people deliberately refrained from talking to each other for long periods, the nature of silence was certainly realised. Abba Poemen, for instance, once said,

> There is one sort of person who seems to be silent, but inwardly criticizes other people. Such a person is really talk-ing all the time. Another may talk from morning to night, but says only what is meaningful, and so keeps silence.[75]

But what was their aim in seeking silence? They wanted to find it so that they could hear, to attend to the voice of God which normally they were too busy, too disturbed, too bathed in noise to hear. In this sense becoming quiet was a crucial part of that form of exploration of inner space which is called prayer, that attention to God, as Simone Weil called it, and to it we shall return in a moment. One of the finest attempts of which I know to express what might happen in silence comes not from the desert, but from a twelfth-century monk, Aelred of Rievaulx, a man much beloved in his day, and by many since. This comes from one of his sermons;

> Your teaching, my good Jesus, is not like that; your waters go with silence. For your teaching, Lord, does not fill the ear with fine-sounding words, but is breathed into the mind by your gentle spirit . . . So, it is heard interiorly, heard in the heart, heard in silence.[76]

It is, I think, of this inward hearing, rather than of hearing the word read in public, that Abba Poemen, again, made one of those remarks which are at once deep and memorable.

> The nature of water is soft, that of stone is hard; but if a bottle is hung above the stone, allowing the water to fall drop by drop, it wears away the stone. So it is with the word of God; it is soft and our heart is hard, but the man who hears the word of God often, opens his heart to the fear of God.[77]

Something can happen, when we are silent. We notice, first, perhaps, the sounds in the room where we sit—the crackling of logs on the fire, the ticking of the clock, the wind at the window. Then we may hear ourselves—the gentle hiss of our breaths, in and out, the rumbling of our digestive system, the beating of our heart, a sound which may be particularly frightening as we grow old. But gradually, if we persist in the quiet, in the exploration of inner space, the strains may fall away, and we become aware of something which we may recognise as a sense of the presence of God, or to which we may give another name, but which is at the time, somehow alive with a silent word for us. This kind of experience was described by George Fox in some of the loveliest and deepest advice which he ever gave:

> Be still and cool in thy own mind and spirit from thine own thoughts, and then thou wilt feel the principle of God to turn thy mind to the Lord God . . .[78]

The desert fathers were clear, too, that the silence may help to keep and preserve afterwards the opening given us in quiet, in other words, to learn when to speak and when to keep silent. Diadochus of Photilei uses a striking simile to make this point:

> When the door of the steambath is continually left open, the heat inside rapidly escapes through it; likewise the soul, in its desire to say many things, dissipates its remembrance of God, through the door of speech, even though everything it says may be good. Thereafter the intellect, though lacking appropriate ideas, pours out a welter of confused thoughts to anyone it meets, as it no longer has the Holy Spirit to keep its understanding free from fantasy. Ideas of value always shun verbosity, being foreign to confusion and fantasy. Timely silence, then, is precious, for it is nothing less than the mother of the wisest thoughts.[79]

These are sobering words to place in any lecture.

There is so much in contemporary life which makes it hard for us to learn to keep silent. Henri Nouwen remarks how awkwardly the emphasis on 'sharing' fits with this side of the teaching of the desert. We should ask ourselves, he suggests,

> whether our lavish ways of sharing are not more compulsive than virtuous; that instead of creating community they tend to flatten out our life together.

I wonder whether this is a point we need to bear in mind? He goes on,

> Often we come home from a sharing session with a feeling that something precious has been taken away for us, or that holy ground has been trodden upon.

Perhaps we need to learn when to be reticent, when to keep silent and to tend the fire silently, and then there may be a word to share.

9 Prayer

At this point it should be clear that in solitude and silence the desert fathers were engaging in forms of prayer, and it is to that subject that I must now turn directly, though with trepidation, because I know how little I know, and that this is an area, perhaps more than any other, where we need to be careful not to speak of more than we know. Again the desert provides us with a striking image:

> A brother came to Abba Theodore and began to converse with him about things which he had never yet put into practice. So the old man said to him, 'You have not yet found a ship nor put your cargo aboard it and before you have sailed, you have already arrived at the city. Do the work first; then you will have the speed you are making now'.[80]

A second danger must be mentioned, too. If it is all too easy to say more about prayer than one knows from experience, to appear to claim something which one has not won in the heart, it is just as easy for those who read or hear words about prayer to listen attentively, to be stirred deeply even, and then to go away and do nothing about the message which had moved them. But there is a seriousness about the call to inward exploration which no one should mess about with.[81] If we are considering moving into that area of experience where we may attend to God, we surely ought to take him seriously. Has he, in no sense feelings? The Bible certainly suggests that he has, and though it proclaims that his thoughts are beyond ours, Jesus and the prophets attributed to him sorrow and pain. This does not seem to be inappropriate to me.

There remains a further problem. No-one attempting to write about prayer for a Quaker, or any other, audience can take for granted that the term will have a generally accepted meaning, nor that there will be universal approval of what the practice involves. It is obvious that the word itself has, for some, unattractive overtones, possibly set up by the experience of taking part in formal public worship, where the repetition of prayer may have seemed mechanical, lifeless and overlong. But there are also those for whom the idea that an individual can address prayer, particularly petition, to God, seems unacceptable because it does not accord with the way that they believe the universe works.[82] Any prayer, for these Friends, which appears to manipulate God, by asking, for example, for the healing of a particular person, is not something in which they can engage because they have formed a nexus of ideas derived from science, philosophy and theology about existence, which leaves no place for prayer. There are also those Friends, who whilst believing in a God with whom the individual may have real contact, feel that any words are totally inappropriate to prayer. As with the issue we met a little earlier, that of the presence of the living Christ, it does not seem right, or feasible, for me here to attempt an extended argument with those who hold such views. Certainly they merit careful and considered discussion, but the last part of a lecture is quite inadequate for it, and I doubt whether my skills are adequate either.[83] Nonetheless, I feel I must indicate in as few words as I can, what my own understanding about prayer is, before trying to pass on some of the things which the desert tradition has to say about it.

I believe that fundamental to the whole coming into existence of the universe is God's desire to have a relationship with people. He seems to have a continuing purpose for the whole of creation, too. That I can not experience, or know, directly, whereas I can be aware that God seems to wish that each of us should freely choose to try to put ourselves alongside his purposes, and to respond to his touch by living in the way which he makes known. Wherever men have opened themselves to the divine, he was there, and their experience and example can teach us and inspire us. The fullest response of which I know to God's purpose was in the life of Jesus, and if I want to know what God's purpose is for me, then I look at God through him, so to say. This means that I believe that the quality of relationship which God has with us, is at least personal.

Prayer, then, is the activity, or place, where we set ourselves to meet God. It is one aspect of our interior space, where, if we attend, we shall be found, we shall know that inward knocking at the door of which Revelation speaks. We meet him too in all we see, in the world, in nature, in people and in our relationships with them. 'The wayfaring ant' of De La Mare's poem, music, painting, sculpture, a loaf of bread, a glass of wine, can also reveal his glory. But I find that I need certain times when I deliberately wait on God, and give him my attention, or else I may be so busy that I miss him. As I wait, it seems to me natural to bring those whom I know to be in need into that inner space, to ask for alleviation of their ills, as well as to offer up my own failures and difficulties, and my thanks and praise. I admit, freely, that I can not prove that my prayer has such and such effects, in the sense of being able to replicate them in a controlled, laboratory situation. But I believe that prayer has changed me, and has enabled me to face situations which I thought might finish me off, though I know that those who know me best might well wonder whether I have grown very much. I have found, too, that when I knew that others were praying for me—when, for example, I fell off my garden wall when pruning and was quite severely damaged—this knowledge was upholding. Yet I know full well that I am but a beginner in the experience of prayer, and need all the help forward that I can get, and, by far the most important thing, need to pray more. I, like many another no doubt, find it easier to read about prayer, or to talk about it, than actually to do it.[84] Indeed I suspect that these things can become an insidious excuse for not setting out on an exciting and difficult journey.

The most helpful thing which the desert fathers say about prayer is about where it is sited, so to speak, where that interior space is. They call it the heart, as when, for example, Macarius said

> The chief task of the athlete [by which he meant the monk] is to enter into the heart.[85]

The same point was made much later by a nineteenth-century Russian, Theophano the Recluse, who lived very much within the desert tradition:

59

To pray is to descend with the mind into the heart, and there
to stand before the face of the Lord, ever-present, all-seeing
within you.[86]

The heart in these and many other passages, does not mean the
area of our personality where feelings arise, but rather the very
centre of our whole being. The word has a meaning consonant
with the whole Judaeo-Christian tradition in which the heart was
held to be 'the source of all physical, emotional, intellectual,
volitional and moral energies.' I would leave it to someone else to
put this in psychological terms, but the concept seems to me to be
near that which we have in our tradition within the term Inner
Light. But it seems clear that if prayer should take place at this
profound level, the centre of ourselves, it cannot be an activity of
the intellect, and so it ought not to be confused with either
thinking about God, nor talking with him.[87] It may be useful to
use an analogy from personal relationships here. When we love
another person, we show our love, not so much by thinking about
them, or by talking to them, but in attentive awareness of them.
There is, of course, a problem; how do we descend into the heart,
to this deep level of ourselves?

Here the answer from the desert seems equally clear: not by a
lot of talk, nor necessarily by spending long periods of time at it.
The crucial thing is desire, being wholly involved in the movement within, holding nothing of ourselves back. The point is
shortly made by Abba Macarius when he answered the question
put to him, 'How should we pray?';

> The old man answered, 'A long speech is not necessary, but
> instead stretch forth your hands and say, "Lord as you know
> and as you wish, have mercy". Yet if you feel a conflict is
> breaking out, you have to say, "Lord, help!" He knows what
> is good for us and treats us accordingly." '[88]

The use of such a dart of prayer in a great public meeting of
Friends occurred in a session of the 1952 World Conference of
Friends at Oxford, when Barrow Cadbury uttered a short prayer

with unforgettable effect.* Now, we perhaps can take Macarius's whole advice into our own practice, and find how helpful the repetition of such a short phrase can be in bringing stillness within. Some may find that merely sitting still silently is better, and this is certainly an area where we differ, and where our practice may vary at different stages in life.[89] The words, or phrase, certainly help me to deal with the distractions which inevitably well up as I pray.

The desert fathers spoke, too, of unceasing prayer, something which Thomas Kelly wrote about most memorably, but the important thing seems to be to begin to set aside a time for prayer every day and to use it, rather than to begin by aiming at something which may arrive in time.[90] Prayer, like many other sides of life, needs a regular discipline. When I have talked of this with Friends, there are always some who are deeply suspicious and feel that one should only pray when the desire to do so arises spontaneously. The desert tradition certainly would disagree, because it recognised that real prayer was not easy: there would be times when it seemed dry and when the one who prayed had to struggle against dark parts of himself.[91] The metaphor of the athlete which we have seen they used, seemed appropriate to them just because they recognised that the journey of self-exploration, of movement into the heart to find God, needed training and education in the fullest sense. No one can learn to love someone else if they only do so when they feel amorous and amiable, when things are going easily; we have to learn to show love in our living. Likewise, if we want to grow in a loving relationship with God, if that is to mean something, we surely need to set aside time and energy for him. The time needed is not huge, Baron von Hügel recommended Evelyn Underhill to spend no more than thirty minutes a day in prayer, and many people have suggested less, but the crucial thing is to make an opportunity to move into our space within.[92]

* 'Oh God we are in a fix please help us out of it'. In *Friends Face the Fourth Century: report of the Third World Conference of Friends, Oxford, July/August, 1952.* FWCC, 1952, p. 78.

The men of the desert realised that the process was not easy and both hinted that in some senses it would become easier, and that it would never be without difficulty. One of the women of the desert, Abba Syncletica, said,

> In the beginning, there is struggle and a lot of work for those who come near God. But after that, there is indescribable joy. It is just like building a fire: at first it's smoky and your eyes water, but later you get the desired result. Thus we ought to light the divine fire in ourselves with tears and effort.[93]

On the other hand, another hermit gave a different answer:

> The brothers asked Abba Agathon, 'Father, which of the virtues in our way of life demands the greatest effort?' He said to them, 'Forgive me, but there is no effort comparable to prayer to God. In fact, whenever you want to pray, hostile demons try to interrupt you. Of course they know that nothing but prayer to God entangles them. Certainly when you undertake any other good work, and persevere in it, you obtain rest. But prayer is a battle all the way to the last breath'.[94]

If any of them had written a treatise on prayer they might have explained the apparent paradox, but I suspect that they were hinting at rhythms and changes which most of those who pray regularly have surely felt. One day the heart seems to be reached very easily, another scarcely at all. Wendy Robinson in a beautiful short exploration of silence, points out that the proper rendering of the Hebrew name for God, translated often 'I am that I am', should be 'I shall be there as I shall be there', which she takes to mean that God's presence is always available to us, but not the form that he will take. She adds,

> If we wish to recognize the form of the Living God in each moment, then we must keep close and be watchful with the love of all our heart, mind and strength. The great forms—-

images—of God were born of encounter, and they change. Thou art this . . . and yet not this . . .[95]

She goes on to quote a prayer by George Appleton, one-time archbishop of Jerusalem, which seems to me so entirely relevant, and in the spirit of the desert tradition that it cries out to be given in full:

O Christ, my Lord, again and again I have said with Mary Magdalene, 'They have taken away my Lord and I know not where they have laid him'. I have been desolate and alone. And thou hast found me again, and I know that what has died is not thou, my Lord, but only my idea of thee, the image which I have made to preserve what I have found, and to be my security. I shall make another image, O Lord, better than the last. That too must go, and all successive images, until I come to the blessed vision of Thyself, O Christ, my Lord.

Solitude, silence and prayer, all bring experiences of peeling away comfortable masks, both those with which we have covered ourselves, and those with which we have hidden ourselves from God.

The desert tradition is, as one might expect, brisk and down-to-earth with those who expect that they will receive special revelations, openings of special wonder. For example;

The devil appeared to a brother, in the disguise of an angel of light, and said to him, 'I am the angel Gabriel and I have been sent to you'. However, the brother said to him, 'See if you are not being sent to someone else. I certainly do not deserve to have an angel sent to me'. Immediately the devil disappeared.[96]

But the aim of all the exercises of the desert, all the disciplines of the monastic life, or of any disciplines which we may adopt for ourselves, is to produce a real change in people, a real transformation. As Benedict put it,

our hearts [and here he was using the word with the sense we have discussed] shall be enlarged, and we shall run with

unspeakable sweetness of love in the way of God's
commandments.[97]

A slightly earlier master living in Asia Minor, Gregory
Nazianzen, put the matter more simply still; the aim was 'To be,
rather than seem to be, a Friend of God'.[98] This is surely an aim in
which we all can unite, whatever formulations we may use when
we talk about God. We seek an authentic experience, because, to
quote Augustine, 'our hearts [the word again] are restless until
they find themselves in thee'.[99] And we sense that it is only as we
are being transformed by God that we become more capable of
responding to the needs of our neighbours. This is not to deny, I
must make clear, that there are many men and women who
respond fully to the needs of others to whom the idea of being
transformed by God would be meaningless. There is much about
the ways of the spirit which we do not understand. But for those to
whom God has made himself known, the feeling of inadequacy,
the sense of a need for transformation is a real one. And for them
the process of growth, of allowing the presence met within to take
a larger part in our lives, of letting our relationship with God
mean more, is sometimes frightening and bewildering. The early
Christians wrote of the fear of the Lord, by which I suppose that
they reflected not merely a well-known Biblical phrase, but the
awareness of being faced by the otherness and holiness of God
which shows up our failings, both those which are trivial and those
which are deep-seated. This kind of experience, as those of loss
and aridity, are those which we may well find it helpful to open to
one another, to ask for help and advice.

The monastic tradition has always had a place for the spiritual
director, or friend, but many Friends find the implications of the
word unattractive. Again and again the desert fathers are shown
helping each other to find new truth, often, as we have seen, with
humour and practical sense. That twelfth-century cistercian,
Aelred, to whom I referred earlier, wrote a short treatise on
Friendship. It reveals its depths with difficulty to the modern
reader, but his whole point is summed up in its opening words,

when Aelred says to his friend,

> 'Here we are, you and I, and I hope a third, Christ, is in our midst'.[100]

Nonetheless I wonder whether we do not need to rediscover the possibilities of a friendship in which the deepest areas of experience may be shared. Certainly that kind of openness seems to have existed in earlier generations among a group who were very significant in the life of the Society. Until this century it was not uncommon for Friends to travel in the ministry, following a real sense of leading in this direction. Often they went out in pairs, one older, one younger. The study of their travels shows, I think, that their friendship became one in which they could open to one another their struggles and failures, their hopes and visions, when they became for each other the way through to the presence of God. On their journeyings, too, they met with Friends in their homes, seeking times for worship and prayer together, sometimes with whole families, sometimes with individuals. In this way they shared help on the inner journey with those with whom they met.[101]

It is this kind of friendship which we need today, to encourage and enrich each other. In my own life, just as the monastic tradition has come to speak to me more relevantly, more to my need in recent years, so have I come to trust other Friends more, and as I have prayed for help, people have made themselves known to whom I can open up. If we are trying to be Friends of God, we can hope we shall find friends on that way. But each of us had different needs, will find help in different ways.

And this leads me to a final word. As I said at the beginning, not everyone who reads this lecture will find it helpful, but there may be some who will, and who may decide to take up some of the suggestions which I have pointed to in the monastic tradition and found helpful myself. I hope no one will be deterred from exploring inner space if they find the going hard, or the methods do not answer their situation. Difficulties are to be expected, because the exploration required is costing, and not all people need the same kind of guides to that exploration, or can use particular practises throughout life. The finding of space, of solitude and silence, a desert for today in which to abide with God, may not be possible, or right for each person at every stage. And God becomes real in so many ways. I know that I have sensed something of his spirit as I have stirred a thickening sauce, or smelt the opening rose, as well as when I have tried to pray. What I believe is crucial, is that each one of us needs to deeply desire to grow into the person whom God wills us to become. Then we can enjoy that quality of life hinted at in a final desert story:

> Abba Lot went to see Abba Joseph and said, 'Abba, as much as I am able I practice a small rule, a little fasting, some prayer and meditation, and remain quiet, and as much as possible I keep my thoughts clean. What else should I do?' Then the old man stood up and stretched out his hands towards heaven, and his fingers became like ten torches of flame. And he said, 'If you wish, you can become all flame'.[102]

The effect may, I suppose, have been made by holding his hand up before the bright sun, but the words surely point towards a different kind of flaming, to Moses sensing the presence in a desert bush, or to the disciples suddenly feeling themselves drawn together by the vivifying spirit. Where better to end, then, than with that great dialogue in the centre of the communion service, which calls towards our very centre, the place where we are held together;

> 'Lift up you hearts'.
> 'We lift them up unto the Lord'.

REFERENCES AND NOTES

[1] William Penn, *No Cross, No Crown* (1682). York: Sessions, rptd. 1981, pp. 63–4, quoted in *Christian Faith and Practice in the Experience of the Society of Friends*. London Yearly Meeting of the Religious Society of Friends, 1960, §395.

[2] *Ibid.*, p. 62.

[3] Cf. the discussion by Justin McCann in his edition and translation of *The Rule of Saint Benedict*. London: Sheed & Ward, 1952, pp. 168, 202–8.

[4] Rufus M. Jones, *The Later Periods of Quakerism*. London: Macmillan, 1921, 2 vols., pp. 39–59; T. E(dmund) Harvey, *Saint Aelred of Rievaulx*. London: Allenson, 1932. For Rufus Jones see my discussion in 'Mystics and Heretics in the Middle Ages: Rufus Jones Reconsidered' in *Journal of the Friends Historical Society*, 53, 1972, pp. 9–30. Douglas Steere's recent *Together in Solitude*. New York, Crossroad, 1982, pursues a number of themes closely allied to those of this lecture.

[5] Thomas F. Green's 1952 Swarthmore Lecture *Preparation for Worship* reflects his life very finely. London: QHS, rptd. 1983.

[6] John A. T. Robinson, *Exploration into God*. London: SCM, 1967, rptd. Oxford: Mowbray, 1977, has a pertinent chapter 'The Journey Inwards'.

[7] David Knowles, *The Evolution of Medieval Thought*. London: Longmans, 1962.

[8] The atmosphere there is well conveyed in Henri J. M. Nouwen, *The Genesee Diary*. New York: Doubleday, Image Books, 1981.

[9] *Psalm 31*, verse 9: I use here Coverdale's translation since it is the most familiar to me because of its presence in the Book of Common Prayer. The *New English Bible* has, at verse 8, 'but thou hast set me free to range at will'.

[10] In the New Children's Edition, London: Macmillan, 1980, pp. 8–11, with two entrancing Tenniel etchings showing Alice moving through.

[11] C. S. Lewis, *The Lion, the Witch and the Wardrobe*. London: Collins, 1950, p. 13.

[12] For discussion of the meaning of the heart see page 60.

[13] A clear and succint presentation of the Rule and its author is in R. W. Southern, *Western Society and the Church in the Middle Ages*. Harmondsworth, Middx.: Penguin, 1970, pp. 218–23. The vast bibliography on these subjects appears in *The Rule of Saint Benedict in Latin and English with Notes* by Timothy Fry, osb and others.

Collegeville, Minn., USA: Liturgical Press, 1981. When I had completed my own text I was introduced to *Seeking God: the way of St. Benedict* by Esther de Waal. London: Fount, 1984. This is a superb 'listening to' the Rule by an Anglican wife, mother and teacher. I wish I had read it sooner.

[14] 'discretione praecipuam, sermone luculentam' in Gregory the Great's *Dialogues*, ii, 36, ed. by U. Moricca. Rome: Fonti per la storia d'Italia, 1924, p. 131.

[15] *The Rule of Saint Benedict* ed. by Justin McCann. London: Sheed & Word, 1952, Prologue, p. 13.

[16] *Church Government*. London Yearly Meeting of the Society of Friends, 1968, rptd. with revisions 1980, §834.

[17] An American Friend, Richard Foster, has not shirked the word in his *Celebration of Discipline*. London: Hodder, 1978. This remarkable book draws on a very wide range of ideas, some from the monastic tradition.

[18] *Church Government*, §702.

[19] *Rule*, 58, p. 131.

[20] *Rule*, 1 for his wandering monks, or gyrovagues, p. 15.

[21] *Christian Faith and Practice*, §376.

[22] *Rule*, 5, 2, 3, pp. 33–5, 17–23, 25 on obedience, the abbot, and taking counsel, are all particularly relevant.

[23] *Rule*, 64, p. 147.

[24] *Rule*, 5, p. 35

[25] *Rule*, 7, pp. 37–49, and see Index, p. 211.

[26] *Rule*, 7, p. 45.

[27] R. S. Surtees, *Mr. Sponge's Sporting Tour* (1853), chapter 34.

[28] From 'Advices', II, in *Church Government*, §702.

[29] *Church Government*, §724.

[30] *Rule*, 8–20, 43, 45, 47, pp. 49–69, 103–5, 107, 109.

[31] *Rule*, 16, p. 61.

[32] *Rule*, 35, 38, 60, pp. 89, 93, 137: there is a lively controversy here to which Fry, *op. cit.*, pp. 410–12 will serve as an entry.

[33] *Rule*, 43, p. 103

[34] *Rule*, 22, p. 71.

[35] Kathleen M. Slack, *Constancy and Change in the Society of Friends*. London: Friends Home Service Committee, 1967, especially pp. 73–9.

[36] *Luke*, 24: 13–32.

STEPS IN A LARGE ROOM

37 Cf. p. 35.
38 *Rule*, 21, 23–30, 65, 69–71, pp. 69–71, 73–81, 149–51, 157–9.
39 *Rule*, 4, pp. 27–33.
40 *Rule*, 72, pp. 159–61.
41 *Rule*, 40, pp. 57.
42 Recognition of this is surely implied by the words which precede the Confession in the Communion Service (1660). 'Ye that do truly and earnestly repent you of your sins, and are in love and charity with your neighbour . . . Draw near in faith . . .' etc.
43 A. A. Milne, *Winnie-the-Pooh*. London: Methuen, 1926, chapter VI, the crux is at pp. 85–7.
44 *John*, 5: 2–9.
45 I can not track this down, so I hope that it is not an invention.
46 *Rule,* 48, p. 111.
47 There is a fine discussion, to which I am much indebted, in Aelred Squire, *Asking the Fathers*. London: SPCK, 1973, chapter 10. The whole book is remarkable. Jean Leclercq, *The Love of Learning and the Desire for God* trns. Catherine Misrahi. London: SPCK, 1978. A superb book; chapter 5 is the source of most of the next two paragraphs.
48 Walter Wink, *Transforming Bible Study*. London: SCM, 1980. His recommendation of writing dialogues (pp. 115–17) would have been well understood in monasteries.
49 Quoted from Squire, *op. cit.,* p. 126.
50 *Moralia in Job*, 2.1, 1; Migne, *Patrologia Latina*, 75, Column 553; I cite here Squire's translation, p. 123.
51 Squire, *op. cit.,* p. 124, translating Migne, 184, column 327–8.
52 *Christian Faith and Practice*. §163: *Early Quaker Writings 1650–1700* ed. by Hugh Barbour and Arthur Roberts. Grand Rapids, Mich., USA: Norfolk Press, 1973, rptd. 1977, p. 258.
53 *Rule*, 18, p. 65: Benedict uses the vulgate numbering, i.e. 4 and 90.
54 Walter Brueggemann, *Praying the Psalms*. Winona, Minn., USA: Pace Book, St Mary's Press, Christian Brothers Publications, 1982. I have also found C. S. Lewis, *Reflections on the Psalms*. London: Fontana, 1960, useful.
55 *New English Bible* version. Oxford University Press and Cambridge University Press, 1961.
56 Brueggemann, *op. cit.,* pp. 40–44.
57 *Ibid.*, pp. 67–79.

58 *Ibid.*, pp. 27–36.

59 *Ibid.*, p. 34.

60 Brueggemann explores 'wings' somewhat differently, pp. 45–8.

61 Brueggemann, *op. cit.,* p. 35, and the next quotation.

62 *Rule*, 73, cf. 42, pp. 161, 101.

63 I use two translations, one by Benedicta Ward, slg, *The Sayings of the Desert Fathers: the Alphabetical Collection.* Oxford: Mowbray, 1975, Cistercian Studies, 59, and the other by Yushi Nomura, *Desert Wisdom: sayings from the Desert Fathers.* London: Eyre & Spottiswood, 1982, a book graced by its simple and witty brush drawings.

64 One of the earliest translations was produced by Helen Waddell, *The Desert Fathers.* London: Constable, 1936.

65 I follow here the general arrangement made by Henri J. M. Nouwen in *The Way of the Heart: Desert Spirituality and Contemporary Ministry.* London: Darton, Longman & Todd, 1981.

66 Derwas Chitty, *The Desert a City: an introduction to the study of Egyptian and Palestinian Monasticism under the Christian Empire.* Oxford: Mowbray, 1966.

67 Ward, *op. cit.,* p. 182 (No. 26).

68 There is a typically balanced discussion of the individualistic character of life in the desert by Henry Chadwick, *The Early Church.* Harmondsworth, Middx.: Penguin, 1967, pp. 174-83.

69 Nomura, *op. cit.,* p. 78.

70 Ward, *op. cit.,* p. 61 (no. 7).

71 Nomura, *op. cit.,* p. 67.

72 Ward, *op. cit.,* p. 120 (no. 7).

73 *Ibid.*, p. 23 (no. 8), quoted by Nouwen, *The Way,* pp. 37–8.

74 See p. 34.

75 Nomura, *op. cit.,* p. 83.

76 Aelred Squire, *Aelred of Rievaulx: a study.* London: SPCK, 1969, p. 67.

77 Ward, *op. cit.,* p. 162 (no. 183), and Nomura, *op. cit.,* p. 59.

78 *Christian Faith and Practice,* §303.

79 Nouwen, *The Way,* pp. 52–3. The words quoted in the next paragraph are from p. 53.

80 Ward, *op. cit.,* p. 64 (no. 9), and Nomura, *op. cit.,* p. 28.

81 Cf. Aelred Squire, *Asking the Fathers,* p. 159: 'To study the question of prayer, without being prepared for what prayer involves, is not only a waste of time; it can be positively harmful . . . We should not

70

experiment with God, or even the devil. It can lead to disaster'.

[82] Eg. Michael Rutter, *A Measure of our Values*. London: Quaker Home Service, 1983, pp. 26–7. A wide variety of views is reflected in *An Exercise of the Spirit: Quakers and Prayer* compiled by Leila Ward, and edited by Ruth W. Bell and Anne Hosking. London: Quaker Home Service, 1984.

[83] Vincent Brümmer, *What are we doing when we pray?* London: SCM Press, 1984, is clear.

[84] Despite the danger, here are some books which I have found helpful: Monica Furlong, *Contemplating Now*. London: Hodder, 1971, Anthony Bloom, *School for Prayer*. London: Darton, 1970, Jack Dobbs, *The Desert and the Market Place*. London: Quaker Home Service, 1984, Wendy Robinson, *Exploring Silence*. Oxford: SLG Press, 1974.

[85] Nouwen, *The Way,* p. 77.

[86] *Ibid.*, p. 76. The next paragraph follows his p. 77.

[87] *Ibid.*, pp. 72–3.

[88] Nomura, *op. cit.*, p. 104, and a slightly different version in Ward, *op. cit.*, p. 111 (no. 19).

[89] Robinson, *op. cit.*, discusses use of touch and sight, pp. 4–6.

[90] Thomas R. Kelly, *A Testament of Devotion* (1943). Rptd. London: Quaker Home Service, 1979.

[91] Cf. Squire, *Asking the Fathers*, p. 149: 'Every beginner in prayer today is likely to need to acquire a healthy distrust of the false contrast that the contemporary world often makes between the value of spontaneity and the danger of habit. The Fathers . . . see the need to value both'.

[92] Steere, *op. cit.*, p. 56. This whole chapter explaining a case of direction is full of insight.

[93] Nomura, *op. cit.*, p. 26.

[94] *Ibid.*, p. 103; Ward, *op. cit.*, pp. 18–9.

[95] Robinson, *op. cit.*, p. 13: the prayer which follows comes on the same page.

[96] Nomura, *op. cit.*, p. 65.

[97] *Rule*, Prologue, p. 13.

[98] *Carmen de vita sua*, 324, and used as a prefatory sentence in Squire, *Asking the Fathers*, p. iv.

[99] *Confessions*, I, chapter 1: 'Fecisti nos ad te et inquietum est cor nostrum, donec requiescat in te'.

[100] *Spiritual Friendship* (Aelred), I, 1, trns. by Mary E. Laker, ssnd, Cistercian Fathers Series, 5. Oxford: Mowbray, 1977, p. 51.

[101] Cf. John Ormerod Greenwood, *Quaker Encounters*, vol 2 *Vines on the Mountains*. York: Sessions, 1977, especially pp. 27–41.

[102] Nomura, *op. cit.,* p. 90: Ward, *op. cit.,* p. 88 (no. 9).